Commitment to Deviance was
composed in Intertype Garamond with
Optima display type by The Book Press,
Brattleboro, Vermont. The entire
book was printed by offset
lithography.

CONTRIBUTIONS IN SOCIOLOGY

Series Editor: Don Martindale

CONTRIBUTIONS IN SOCIOLOGY, NUMBER 5

COMMITMENT TO DEVIANCE

THE NONPROFESSIONAL CRIMINAL IN THE COMMUNITY

ROBERT A. STEBBINS

GREENWOOD PUBLISHING CORPORATION
WESTPORT, CONNECTICUT

TO KARIN

Library of Congress Catalog Card Number: 75-95504
SBN: 8371-2339-9

Greenwood Publishing Corporation
51 Riverside Avenue, Westport, Connecticut 06880

Printed in the United States of America

CONTENTS

TABLES

ACKNOWLEDGMENTS

Expressions of appreciation are due members of the staff at Her Majesty's Penitentiary, the Salmonier Prison Camp, the Harbour Grace Gaol, all in Newfoundland, and Dorchester Penitentiary, New Brunswick. These people suffered through the unavoidable disruption of routine while I carried out the interviews. This study could not have been completed had not their cooperation been the rule throughout. I have also benefited from a small travel grant received from the Vice-President's Research Fund at Memorial University. It made the second phase of this investigation possible.

Several of my colleagues at Memorial University and elsewhere politely endured the task of critically reading the early drafts of this book. I am deeply indebted to Jean Briggs, Robert DeWitt, Lorna Holbrook Mui, and John Nicholson for undertaking this less than pleasant job. Professor Don Martindale has also contributed to the overall quality of this work through his helpful editorial comments. Unfortunately, any errors, omissions, or misconceptions found in this monograph cannot be charged to these readers; I alone am culpable in these instances.

Karin Y. Stebbins shouldered the double burden of maintaining family equilibrium while I devoted myself to the manuscript, and typing the final draft. Her contributions to the completion of this work are inestimable.

I also gratefully acknowledge the authors and publishers who gave permission to use their materials in this book:

American Sociological Association: from "History, Culture and Subjective Experience: An Exploration of the Social Bases of Drug-Induced Experiences" by Howard S. Becker, from *The Journal of Health and Social Behavior,* September 1967. By permission of the author and the American Sociological Association.

The Bobbs-Merrill Co., Inc.: from *The Effectiveness of a Prison and Parole System* by Daniel Glaser, copyright © 1964, by The Bobbs-Merrill Company, Inc., reprinted by permission of the publishers.

The Canadian Press: from "Teen-age Crime Returns to Haunt Man" by The Canadian Press, 18 January 1967.

Hutchinson & Co.: from *The Courage of His Convictions* by Tony Parker and Robert Allerton, copyright © 1962, by Hutchinson & Co., reprinted by permission of the publishers.

McGraw-Hill Book Co.: from *Social Pathology* by Edwin M. Lemert. Copyright 1951 by McGraw-Hill Book Co. Used with permission of McGraw-Hill Book Company, Inc.

Prentice-Hall, Inc.: from Edwin M. Lemert, *Human Deviance, Social Problems, and Social Control,* © 1967, Prentice-Hall, Inc., Englewood Cliffs, New Jersey.

United States Courts: from "The Anticriminal Society: Synanon" by Lewis Yablonsky, from *Federal Probation,* September 1962. Reprinted by permission of the author and the United States Courts.

The University of Chicago Press: from *The Professional Thief* by Edwin Sutherland by permission of the University of Chicago Press, copyright 1937; from *The Jack Roller,* by Clifford Shaw by permission of The University of Chicago Press, copyright 1930; from "Reformation and Recidivism among Italian and Polish Criminal Offenders" by Harold Finestone, from *The American Journal of Sociology,* May 1967, by permission of The University of Chicago Press, copyright 1967.

John Wiley & Sons, Inc.: from *Wayward Puritans* by Kai T. Erikson. Copyright 1966 by John Wiley & Sons, Inc. Reprinted by permission of John Wiley & Sons, Inc.

INTRODUCTION

Around noon one day, late in 1966, residents of St. John's, Newfoundland, were surprised to hear the sound of gunfire as guards from Her Majesty's Penitentiary attempted to halt three inmates trying to escape. The break was not serious for none of the three were armed or considered dangerous; in fact, two of them were recaptured later that very afternoon. The third, William (Fox) Williams, remained at large for several weeks until he was finally discovered in a lonely shack on the southeastern edge of the city.

On the front page of its January 16, 1967 edition, *The Evening Telegram*, a major St. John's newspaper, carried an exclusive interview with the recaptured inmate:

> William (Fox) Williams, 23, says he is "punished both inside and outside the penitentiary."
>
> In an interview with *The Telegram* Friday he said that while he is on the outside he can't get a job "because too many people know me, and on the inside I'm kept in confinement most of the time."

He said: "After this I'll be transferred to Dorchester Penitentiary and when I get out I won't be returning here anymore. Nothing will get me back."

The six-foot resident of Ridge Road, St. John's, said that in 1966 he had returned home after serving a three-year term at Dorchester Federal Penitentiary in New Brunswick.

"I learned a trade in upholstering during my time there. It's a good trade but there is no work in this province for it, at least not for me.

"When I got out, I didn't want to come back here, but I was married and decided I should. This fell apart and I wanted to get out [of the province].

"I tried for a job but everyone here knows me or has heard of me and I just couldn't get work. I tried to go straight to get enough money to get out of the province but I wasn't given a chance.

"This time when my time's done I'm staying on the mainland where no one knows me and I'm going to go straight."

Two days later the same newspaper reported a different incident involving a town councillor in New Waterford, Nova Scotia.

A car theft in Toronto nearly 10 years ago returned to haunt a New Waterford town councillor—and he has been forced to resign his position as a result of it.

Murray Tait, at 26 the youngest man ever elected to town council here, resigned Tuesday night after his eligibility to hold the seat was questioned by the man he defeated in the December municipal election.

Gordon McInnes presented a document to Mayor Dan Nathanson showing Mr. Tait had been convicted in Toronto as a teen-ager on a charge of theft.

"I made the protest," Mr. McInnes said. "I have no other comment other than that I will not be a candidate in any by-election."

Mr. McInnes lost to Mr. Tait by 119 votes in the December election.

"I am extremely distressed by this situation," the mayor said. "However, having conferred with the town solicitor there doesn't seem to be any course left but to accept the resignation.

"Persons convicted of any crime punishable by a term in a penitentiary are ineligible to hold office in Nova Scotia."

Mr. Tait, father of three, admitted he was convicted on the theft charge in Toronto. He said he was 17 at the time and was fined $200.

"This happened in Toronto a long time ago. I was a passenger in a car that was stolen by a group of teen-agers. At the time we thought it was just a lark. We were all young and regretted our action at the time."

Municipal Affairs Minister Donald C. MacNeil said Tuesday night he will take immediate steps to investigate the "propriety of what may be antiquated law."

Four months later, almost to the day, a similar experience befell a federal Member of Parliament who had held that position for ten years.

Incidents such as these raise a number of questions. What are the chances of gaining a respectable position in the community for men who have been in prison? What factors militate against their return to conventional life? Will their criminal records someday return to haunt them in the manner experienced by the two politicians mentioned above? These questions all concern the later stages of the deviant career, one of the aspects of the study of deviance that is particularly underdeveloped.

In the following chapters a general theory of forced behavior, or of "continuance commitment," as Rosabeth Kanter has recently phrased it, is developed to help account for the behavior observed during this part of the deviant career. Central to this theory is the idea that commitment can explain the relationships between the publicly known deviant and members of the community. Commitment is the belief on the part of the committed individual that he is trapped in his deviant role by the force of penalties that appear when he tries to establish himself in nondeviant circles. Recognition of these penalties marks a major turning point in his deviant career; one where his realization of the forces both for and against continued deviance is especially acute. While they are by no means mutually exclusive in their meaning, as we shall see, this concept of commitment is to be distinguished from value commitment or the positive attraction to a specified belief, attitude, or pattern of behavior.

Although we are mainly concerned with deviance in this study, I have taken the opportunity in Chapter 2 to present a more general theory of commitment. In this theory a person may become committed to a specific expectation of behavior, in which case commitment refers to the pressure to continue to carry out this expectation. Or a person may become committed to a particular deviant or nondeviant identity (considered as a constellation of expectations). Here commitment refers to the pressure to remain in that status. The pressure to maintain a line of behavior results from the existence of penalties fostered by specific arrangements in life, such as the privileges of seniority in a business firm, the irreversible investment of time, energy, and money in obtaining a medical degree, or the addiction to a drug. These three illustrative arrangements can potentially generate social, psychological, and biological penalties, respectively, for the person who wishes to abandon one firm for another, for the disenchanted physician who would really prefer to be a professional musician, or for the addict who wants to "get the monkey off his back." The loss of the privileges of seniority by bureaucratic fiat is penalizing; the loss of the benefit of the invested time, energy, and money in education is psychologically distressing since it cannot be reclaimed; the penalizing nature of withdrawal pains can be corroborated by any addict who has tried to kick the habit "cold turkey." Another precondition of commitment is that the cost or penalty be perceived by the person as imminent, in the sense of having a high probability of occurrence either immediately or at some recognized time in the future. It is the imminence of the penalties that creates an awareness in the individual of his growing commitment to a particular line of behavior.

Commitment is not necessarily a negative phenomenon. When an individual finds an attractive self-conception in the identity he is forced to retain, or in the expectation of behavior he is required to play out, we may speak of "self-enhancing" commitment. When a negative self-image is involved, we may speak of "self-degrading" commitment. In either case it is possible that the imminent threat of certain penalties is what compels the person to sustain a particular pattern of behavior, whether he desires to change it or not.

People do not become committed to a given identity or given expectation of behavior at the same rate, and it is easier to avoid commitment to some identities than to others. One of the factors behind this situation is the observation that there are differences in the inevitability of the various kinds of penalties. That is, because some penalties, such as ridicule or ostracism, do not occur with the same degree of regularity as other kinds, such as the withdrawal stress mentioned above, commitment will develop at a differential rate depending upon the identity (and the penalties associated with it) under consideration. Furthermore, commitment is often of limited duration. Thus self-degrading commitment, because it is undesirable, motivates the individual to try various strategies to escape this condition, whereas in the self-enhancing form this is not likely to happen.

One of the weaknesses of the theory of commitment is the lack of empirical knowledge about the nature of the penalties that threaten those who wish to abandon their deviant identities. In order to shed some light on this class of penalties and their relationship to the process of commitment, an exploratory study comprised of two sets of interviews was undertaken. The first of these, carried out in September and October of 1967, concerned twenty-two third- and fourth-time property offenders then incarcerated in Her Majesty's Penitentiary in St. John's, Newfoundland. These offenders, selected as representative of "nonprofessional criminals," are believed to experience a variety of social penalties and few, if any, psychological or biological penalties. This sets them apart from other kinds of deviants, such as homosexuals or narcotics addicts, who also suffer nonsocial penalties like sexual deprivation or withdrawal pains when they try to reject their disreputable statuses.

In order to discover how the penalties arising from the attempted rejection of a deviant identity vary, a sample of nineteen professional criminals was also interviewed. It was hypothesized that while professional criminals are, objectively speaking, committed to their role, they are less aware of potential penalties since their ideological attachment to their way of life makes it unlikely that they would want to abandon it. This part of the investigation, carried out in December 1968, in Dorchester Federal Penitentiary in New Brunswick, discloses that most of the professional criminals interviewed have little or no conscious awareness of the penalties experienced by the nonprofessional criminals who attempt to reenter the wider community.

The findings of this study are phrased as penalties experienced by the nonprofessional criminals in their attempts to reestablish themselves in the community. Since this investigation is largely exploratory in nature, each penalty that received sufficient support is summarized as a hypothesis for future research. Some of the hypothetical penalties that emerged are presented below:

1. A nonprofessional criminal with a known prison record will have difficulty finding a job within his personal range of acceptable alternatives.
2. When a nonprofessional criminal with a known prison record does find a job, it will be at the lower end of the occupational prestige spectrum.
3. Being questioned by casual acquaintances about aspects of one's criminal life is an unsettling experience for the nonprofessional criminal.
4. Curiosity and recognition stares aimed at the nonprofessional criminal by nondeviant members of the community are odious to him.
5. While interacting with others who are unaware of his deviant identity, the nonprofessional criminal meets unanticipated requests to disclose information about himself that he feels to be discrediting.
6. In neutral company, the nonprofessional criminal

opens himself up to the possibility of hearing the often humiliating truth about how nondeviant others view people like himself.

In the final chapter the implications of the findings for prisoner aftercare and public policy are briefly examined. Although the results are tentative, they point, for instance, to the importance of eradicating criminal records after a period of time and to the belief that for nonprofessional offenders less newspaper and other mass media coverage of their activities will facilitate their reentry into the wider community. This inquiry concludes with a short discussion of commitment as a cause of deviance and the research design required to implement an investigation of this nature.

1

THE DEVIANT CAREER

Over fifteen years have passed since Edwin Lemert presented his comprehensive statement of the theory of sociopathic behavior in *Social Pathology*. Although the theory has not received nearly the amount of attention it warrants, considering its excellence, it has still been the basis for a good deal of research and further theorizing in the study of deviance. Fundamentally, it is a sociological and social-psychological model.[1] Deviance is seen as resulting from macrosociological factors of a social structural and cultural nature and from microsociological factors such as the interaction between the deviant and conventional others and attempts to validate a particular self-conception. Factors falling outside this range of variables, where they have been demonstrated to influence the development of deviance, must be related to them. Any discussion of effective causation is limited to the sociological and social-psychological levels.

Because of its central importance to the themes to be

developed in this monograph, it is necessary to spell out some of Lemert's ideas in detail so that we may build upon them in later chapters.

THE THEORY OF
SOCIOPATHIC BEHAVIOR

Although the total theory is considerably more detailed and complex, the following summary statement by Lemert will be sufficient for our purposes.

> We start with the idea that persons and groups are differentiated in various ways, some of which result in social penalties, rejection, and segregation. These penalties and segregative reactions of society or the community are dynamic factors which increase, decrease, and condition the form which the initial differentiation or deviation takes. This process of deviation and societal reaction, together with its structural or substantive products, can be studied both from its collective and distributive aspects. In the first instance, we are concerned with sociopathic differentiation; and, in the second, our concern is with sociopathic individuation.[2]

There are three important aspects to this theory which receive a great deal of further elaboration in Lemert's book. The first of these, the process of differentiation, refers to the fact that people differ or deviate from average characteristics of the populations in which they are found and in which they interact. The second is the societal reaction which indicates "both the expressive reactions of others (moral indignation) toward deviation and action directed to its control."[3] Of course, it depends upon the deviant individual or class of individuals being visible enough to react to. Individuation is the third aspect of the theory, and it refers to the manifestation of the causes of deviance in the individual deviant and to how he comes to grips with his fate.

This framework is then given a more substantive form by being incorporated into a body of postulates:

1. There are modalities in human behavior and clusters of deviations from these modalities which can be identified and described for situations specified in time and space.

2. Behavioral deviations are a function of culture conflict, and such conflict is expressed through social organization.

3. There are societal reactions to deviations ranging from strong approval through indifference to strong disapproval.

4. Sociopathic behavior is deviation which is *effectively* disapproved.

5. The deviant person is one whose role, status, function, and self-definition are importantly shaped by how much deviation he engages in, by the degree of its social visibility, by the *particular* exposure he has to the societal reaction, and by the nature and strength of the societal reaction.

6. There are patterns of restriction and freedom in the social participation of deviants which are related directly to their status, role, and self-definitions. The biological strictures upon social participation of deviants are directly significant in comparatively few cases.

7. Deviants are individuated with respect to their vulner-

ability to the societal reaction because: (*a*) the person is a dynamic agent, (*b*) there is a structuring to each personality which acts as a set of limits within which the societal reaction operates.[4]

Lemert does not intend this set of postulates to be exhaustive or that all of them are even relevant to the focus of his theory. This, he says, must be determined by future research.

INDIVIDUATION

It is the process of individuation that concerns us most in this study and, consequently, that part of Lemert's theory on which we must spend considerable time. For it is this notion which is related to the rise of a new approach to the study of deviance, an approach consolidated in the ideas of the deviant career and the labeling of deviants.

The concept of individuation can be understood best by looking at the events and processes associated with "primary deviation" and "secondary deviation." The first of these refers to the kind of deviant behavior which is normalized by its perpetrator. That is, "the deviations remain primary deviations or symptomatic and situational as long as they are rationalized or otherwise dealt with as functions of a socially acceptable role." [5] In a later book Lemert explains that "this is done either through *normalization,* in which the deviance is perceived as normal variation—a problem of everyday life —or through management and nominal controls which do not seriously impede basic accommodations people make to get along with each other." [6] Secondary deviation refers to the responses which people make to problems created by the societal reaction to their deviance. These problems are those which are generated by social control mechanisms, punishment, stigmatization or labeling, segregation, and the like. They are of exceptional importance to the individual in that they alter his personality. "The secondary deviant . . . is a person whose life and identity are organized around the facts of deviance." [7]

Lemert expresses the relationship between primary and secondary deviation in the following way:

> The sequence of interaction leading to secondary deviation is roughly as follows: (1) primary deviation; (2) social penalties; (3) further primary deviation; (4) stronger penalties and rejections; (5) further deviation, perhaps with hostilities and resentment beginning to focus upon those doing the penalizing; (6) crisis reached in the tolerance quotient, expressed in formal action by the community stigmatizing of the deviant; (7) strengthening of the deviant conduct as a reaction to the stigmatizing and penalties; (8) ultimate acceptance of deviant social status and efforts at adjustment on the basis of the associated role.[8]

This relationship between primary and secondary deviation just described can, with little difficulty, be incorporated into the idea of deviant career.

The Deviant Career

The notion of career is borrowed from the sociology of occupations where it has been defined as the movement of a person through a series of positions within some sort of occupational system.[9] In the study of deviance it has become the mainspring of a new approach often referred to as the "labeling approach" because of its emphasis on the career contingency or career turning point of stigmatization by the community for one's past actions.

Objectively, it is the initial act of deviance that launches the individual's deviant career. However, as we shall see in the next chapter, career contingencies including this one depend upon the actor's recognition and interpretation of them before they can be considered as part of a career. This is usually evident only in retrospect after one has spent a certain amount of time in the identity with which the career is associated. Thus, upon reflection (usually stimulated by some current turning point) the first remembered act of homosexuality, the first interest in Communist literature, or the first drag on a marihuana cigarette constitutes the inception of the person's deviant career. This may or may not be the initial instance of deviance from a more objective point of view. This act and those further acts of primary deviation which may or may not follow are the result of many factors —social, cultural, psychological, and physiological—and their manifold combinations.[10] Of course, any discussion of deviance should not overlook the possibility of false accusation of deviant behavior, an event which can also, under the proper circumstances, lead to a subsequent deviant career.

Becker has suggested three types of deviants (primary deviants for us) which can be distinguished at this career point of one or a few deviant acts.[11] There is the "secret deviant" whose behavior is not, to his knowledge, known beyond himself and perhaps a few others. The "falsely accused" deviant, whether this attitude is in fact valid or not, believes in his own innocence. The falsely accused deviant is also a discovered deviant in the sense that he has been apprehended for or suspected of deviant behavior. Finally, there is the "pure deviant" who is also a discovered deviant since he has behaved in an aberrant way, knows it, and has been apprehended for or suspected of such activity by certain members of the larger community.

It should suffice, for the time being, to point out that each of these types is founded in the deviant person's own view of himself and not in the sociologist's view or the community's view. Although we may have taken some liberty with Becker's classification in doing so, this modification of it in favor of the deviant's perspective is preferred since a subjective orientation is to be used throughout this book.

Interaction With the Agents of Social Control

The amount and kinds of interaction that take place between the individual who is suspected of deviant behavior (a discovered deviant) and the representatives of the agencies of social control is extremely important for the future course of that person's deviant career. In fact, the events that take place here make up a set of career contingencies: those factors on which mobility from one position to another depends.

Cohen has stated this process most clearly: alter (the agents of social control) responds to the action of ego (the deviant); ego in turn responds to alter's reaction; alter then responds to his perception of ego's reaction to him; and so forth. The final result is that ego's opportunity structure is in some way modified, permitting either greater or lesser legitimate or illegitimate opportunities.[12]

Where the opportunities for a deviant career have been expanded, the process is one of "schizmogenesis," the steady growing apart of two parties which culminates in open conflict.[13] Some proportion of these encounters lead in the opposite direction, however, culminating in some form of accommodation and a decrease in the opportunities for a deviant career.

The author recalls one schizmogenic series of encounters reported by one of the respondents interviewed in this study. The respondent arrived in Toronto shortly after being released from prison in New Brunswick, only to be stopped while walking on a main street by two policemen in a prowl car. He was apparently immediately recognized and advised to return to his home province without further delay. But since he had just come from there, the respondent politely informed the police that he had important business in Toronto which would take a few days to accomplish, and after that he would consider leaving the city. This was not the sort of reaction the police were after, so they pressed their request again in a firmer manner. The respondent's reply was likewise more adamant, and the police left without success. That evening he was called from his rented room by his landlady only to be confronted by two different but "enormous" policemen who had just arrived in an ominous-looking police van. They again questioned him about his intentions to stay in Toronto, but the respondent, who could now see that he would probably remain in that city only in jail, replied that he had decided to return to New Brunswick after all.

This process of interaction underlies four different stages of the relationship between the pure or falsely accused deviant and the agents of social control. The first stage is that of discovery, which we have already discussed, where the person is first apprehended because he is suspected of a deviant act. He may be arrested if the norm violated is a formal one, or he may simply be observed directly or indirectly by members of the community. Discovery leads to "confrontation" of the individual by the agents of social control, as in the criminal trial or the psychiatric interview.[14] After confrontation, the pure or falsely accused deviant must face some sort of "judgment." It may be a formal verdict or a diagnosis, or it may be an informal summing up of evidence by the accused violator's neighbors or companions. Whatever the case, he is labeled at this point by the community or its official representatives. Finally, providing the judgment is that of guilty, the now publicly known deviant must undergo "placement." He takes on a new status, such as prisoner, patient, or, if informally dealt with, simply outcast. This change usually has profound personal consequences, and it is one that frequently involves a corresponding change in self-conception.[15] Often it happens that these stages occur informally sometime before the official sequences of confrontation, judgment, and placement, making the formal encounter, if it ever takes place, a sort of hollow exercise because it deals with preordained outcomes. Thus, the police and even the citizens of the community may be convinced of a person's criminal activities before an actual arrest and trial take place.[16]

Furthermore, official labeling may not have the effect of a negative societal reaction at all, at least in some parts of the community. Subcultural groups occasionally evaluate treatment of one of their members by the larger community agents of social control in ways strikingly different from those of the dominant segment. The institution of vendetta among Chicago Italians during the early part of this century, while regarded as wanton killing by indigenous Americans, was seen by the Italians as part of their way of life, murder as vengeance being thought of as a ritual obligation to a previously murdered kinsman. The sympathetic reaction of jazz musicians to the arrest and conviction of one of their fellows for the use of marihuana is another example of this sort of reaction to the official labeling of deviants.

It is instructive to add to the catalogue of types of deviants what might be called the *acquitted-suspected deviant:* the individual who is suspected of a deviant act but who is exonerated of the charge. His deviant career ends, at least temporarily, at the judgment stage of the interaction with the community agents of social control. Depending on how the community perceives the validity of the acquittal decision, the acquitted-suspected deviant could suffer a certain amount of dishonor and be forced into or committed to the role of a semideviant. Schwartz and Skolnick provide evidence of this kind of response to the individual exonerated in this way:

> Another important finding of this study concerns the small number of positive responses elicited by the "accused but acquitted" applicant. Of the twenty-five employers approached with this folder, three offered jobs. Thus, the individual accused but acquitted of assault has almost as much trouble finding even an unskilled job as the one who was not only accused of the same offense, but also convicted.[17]

The judgment stage of the interaction between the deviant and the agents of social control is generally the point in the deviant's career at which he becomes labeled or stigmatized. This necessarily precedes the societal reaction which is manifested in placement of some kind. Of course, for some deviants who make the full transition from primary to secondary forms of deviance, this phase of the interaction with the agents of social control recurs several times with increasing severity of outcome each time.

There are a number of factors that influence the interaction between the discovered deviant and the agents of social control in the discovery, confrontation, and judgment stages. In this connection Cohen has made the observation that Merton's types of adaptation to anomie can also be conceptualized in terms of responses to deviant behavior. Thus, officials may innovate (e.g., McCarthyism, third-degree methods), be ritualistic (e.g., preoccupation with the minutiae of procedure without regard to effectiveness in reaching an end), retreat (e.g., refusal to concern oneself with the fact of deviant behavior), or rebel (e.g., acceptance of the deviant's goals and means of reaching them, as seen in corrupt policemen).[18] As we are employing them here, these responses are not societal or community reactions to categories of deviants but the reactions of individual officials to individual deviants. They take place in the discovery, confrontation, and judgment stages of the deviant's career.

Becker points out still other factors relevant in these phases of the deviant's career.[19] The officials appointed by society to enforce its rules occasionally must show that they are doing their job in order to justify their position. Furthermore, since these enforcement agents are often in a position to choose whether or not to arrest or apprehend an individual, any misbehavior on the latter's part may bring forth a harsher reaction than might deference. Also, there is always the possibility of the "fix," which is actually a form of rebellion in Cohen's terms. Finally, the rule enforcers may develop their own private set of priorities with respect to which kinds of violation are most important, priorities which may diverge from the set held by the community as a whole.[20]

The societal reaction in the placement stage is an extremely complicated matter. We have already postulated that it varies by the amount of deviance engaged in and the degree of visibility of that deviance. It also varies extensively within modern industrial societies along the lines of certain social class and religious variables and with respect to the kind of deviance under consideration. Thus, middle-class members of one community were found by Rooney and Gibbons to hold a relatively favorable attitude toward abortion seekers, while maintaining a more hostile stance toward homosexuals and drug users. The same study, as might be expected, showed Roman Catholics to be less tolerant of the practice of abortion than Protestants.[21] Erikson has demonstrated that deviance is influenced by the sociohistorical context in which it takes place.[22] What the Puritans defined as religious deviance in their day is not even an issue today. Deviance has been shown to vary widely from one culture to another when its form is held constant. Lemert, who includes stutterers within his definition of deviance, observed that among the Hawaiians and the Samoans such people are not socially rejected and they do not withdraw from society.[23] Furthermore, the societal reaction manifests itself in many ways, from various degrees of acceptance and rejection to the many forms of punishment, methods of control, and strategies for removal which differ as widely as societies themselves.

In what is fundamentally a discussion of career contingencies at the placement stage, Parsons, in his presentation of deviance from a dyadic point of view, indicates that alter's disposition may be such that he is driven to impose unduly harsh sanctions on ego as a defense against his own repressed deviant wishes.[24] This exaggerated punishment may only further alienate ego: it may be a contingency which helps advance his deviant career. Also, the deviant may be treated or punished in a way that is in harmony with the popular diagnosis of why he behaved in a deviant manner in the first place.[25] For instance, the drug addict is conventionally seen as being weak-willed. The proper corrective for such behavior, so far as popular thought goes, is to deny him his pleasures by making it illegal to possess narcotics. One is reminded of the early folklore surrounding crime and mental illness in which criminals and the insane were believed to be possessed by demons, the only cure being diurnal floggings and similar measures designed to drive these devilish spirits from the body by making it too uncomfortable to remain there. Such treatment may only increase the probability of an extended deviant career since legitimate opportunities may have been restricted as a result of it.

Whatever happens in the interaction between the pure or falsely accused deviant and the representatives of the institutions of social control, it is certain that this set of contingencies will have an effect on two other sets of deviant career contingencies: the deviant's interaction with conventional members of the community and his interaction with other deviants.

Interaction Between the Publicly Known Deviant and the Conventional Members of the Community

Beyond the deviant's contact with the agents of social control, there is still another important contingency in the interaction between him and the conventional members of the community: the difficulties encountered by the publicly known deviant in attempting to return to conventional life.

At some time in his career it is often the case that the deviant wishes to desert the world of the discredited for an attempt to live a conventional life. A religious cultist may, for example, wish to abandon his beliefs for more commonly acceptable ones; a homosexual may seek psychiatric help for his affliction; a heroin addict may try to "kick" the habit for good.

How successful a conventional career will be after one has been labeled a deviant, even if he has committed only one alienating act, is a question for research. Perhaps he will be forced into or committed to the marginal status of semideviant.[26] Whatever the reasons, it seems plausible to hypothesize that the longer the deviant career and the more publicly known and seriously regarded the deviant's acts, the more difficult it is to reenter conventional life, although at least partially successful entry is by no means impossible.[27]

Nevertheless, there are certain qualifying conditions to this proposition. There is some evidence that hospitalization for mental illness can have the effect of *halting* certain processes of alienation while stimulating processes of reintegration within the family.[28] Furthermore, it has been shown that community status can be a significant variable, especially when accompanied by such factors as the public need for a particular service and the support from professional and other organizations.[29] It may be easier, other things being equal, to gain admittance to the conventional world if one's educational and occupational statuses are highly respected than if they are not.

At least two other variables are also seen as qualifying this hypothesis about reentering conventional life. Becker,

in *Outsiders,* has suggested that part of the difficulty encountered in attempting to return to conventional life is related to the fact that being a deviant is a master status and
that it has certain master and auxiliary traits. The position
of deviant in our culture is one which is often the most important identity such a person has, and this identity carries
with it certain expected traits, though they may not actually
be present. Becker presents some of the effects of the master
traits associated with the convicted (and therefore labeled)
housebreaker. It is reasoned by conventional members of the
community that if the person in question burglarizes a house
once he might well do it again and, consequently, he should
be watched. The police are typically guided by this belief,
knowing the recidivist rates; they make it a practice to round
up known ex-offenders who, in the light of their past deviant
records, could have possibly been involved in a specific
housebreaking. More than one respondent in the present
study mentioned that occasionally "squares" were cautious
when he was present, lest he take something of value belonging to them. The nature of the deviant position and these
ancillary traits often have the effect of blocking passage
back to acceptance by the community.

Additionally, while there is often a clear set of rites
of passage from the status of conventional member of the
community to that of deviant, there is seldom any corresponding set to help the deviant work his way back, if he
should happen to want to do this.[30] In Erikson's words:
"the deviant often returns home with no proper license to
resume a normal life in the community." He is not recognized as having changed from his dishonorable state.

In a very real way those difficulties encountered by the

deviant when trying to resume life in the larger community as a so-called normal citizen act to facilitate his pursuit of a deviant career. In many cases the members of the wider community are not ready to accept the reformed deviant, a fact which he soon learns in interaction with them in a variety of different social situations. Life in the conventional world can be a painful series of failures or only partial successes and, when contrasted with the seemingly warm and understanding deviant subculture, it is no wonder that a deviant career is chosen over one in the community as a whole. Life may be risky here, as in the case of criminals and narcotics addicts, but socially and psychologically it is often more tolerable. We shall return to these ideas in the following chapters.

Interaction Between the Publicly Known Deviant and Other Deviants

The process of interaction between *ego and other deviants* is often from the outset an important factor. However, no success or a perceived low probability of success in attaining respectability among nondeviants often leads, it seems, to further (or possibly initial) interaction with other deviants.[31] We are considering here a special aspect of this sort of interaction, interaction which takes place between the publicly known deviant and the organized deviant group. There are several characteristics of this type of group life which stimulate or maintain such behavior, and they are effective partly because the wider community has rejected the deviant.

As Becker has pointed out, the individual who has gained entrance to a deviant group often learns from it how to cope with the various problems associated with deviance.

This makes being a deviant easier. Furthermore, he acquires rationalizations for his values, attitudes, and behavior which come to full bloom in the organized group. While these rationalizations are highly varied, it is important for our purposes to note that their very existence seems to point to the fact that many deviants feel a need to deal with certain conventional attitudes and values which they have also internalized.[32] Becker's recent discussion of the incipient development of a drug culture associated with the problems of LSD use demonstrates the teaching function of the deviant group:

> Users with some experience discuss their symptoms and translate from one idiosyncratic description into another, developing a common conception of effects as they talk. The notion that a "bad trip" can be brought to a speedy conclusion by taking thorazine by mouth (or, when immediate action is required, intravenously) has spread. Users are also beginning to develop a set of safeguards against committing irrational acts while under the drug's influence. Many feel, for instance, that one should take one's "trip" in the company of experienced users who are not under the drug's influence at the time; they will be able to see you through bad times and restrain you when necessary. A conception of the appropriate dose is rapidly becoming common knowledge.[33]

Another important dimension of the interaction between a deviant and members of the organized deviant group is the phenomenon of group conformity. Krech and his associates define conformity in the following way: "The yielding of the individual's judgment or action to group pressure arising from a conflict between his own opinion and that maintained by the group."[34] Certain situational factors

are said to govern the amount of conformity.[35] Group com-
position is important where there are perceived differences
in status and competency. For example, a communist anxious
to gain a favorable reputation in the local party organization
will find that he must conform more than a high-ranking
member. High group consensus on a given issue may insure
greater conformity than low group consensus. The strength
of coercive measures available to the group as a whole is
also significant. The techniques for ensuring conformity to
subgroup ideals among incarcerated prisoners are well
known and include knifings, beatings, and ostracism. Often
prison officials can prevent these occurrences only by isolat-
ing the potential victim, such as by placing him in the prison
hospital. In addition to these points, a number of individual
factors are related to the degree of conformity, among which
should be mentioned the degree of internalization of deviant
group values.

Because group forces operate to maintain and even promote deviance, it should not be assumed, as Goffman apparently does,[36] that full-fledged deviants are always members of such groups. As we shall point out in subsequent
chapters, there are some who reject the label of deviant during
some phases of their career although they may be committed
to that status. Some of these individuals spend part of their
career trying to reenter conventional life, often without success.
Yet, the fact that they do not identify themselves as deviant
leads them at times to avoid others who also are so labeled.[37]
There are, moreover, some forms of deviant behavior which
for one reason or another require isolation. The rapist is an
example and so are some mentally ill persons.[38] It is probably
true, nevertheless, that deviance has collective support in more
cases than not.

SUMMARY AND CONCLUSIONS

The theory of sociopathic behavior focuses on three major processes: the differentiation of deviant behavior from average behavior, the societal reaction to this form of activity, and the individuation or manifestation of the causes of deviance in the person. Individuation is best seen in the events and processes associated with primary and secondary deviation. The former refers to the way of dealing with the fact of one's deviance by means of the everyday adjustment mechanisms present in the standard behavioral repertoire. The latter signifies the reaction of the person for whom deviance has become a primary fact, disrupting most or all of his daily activities.

The transition from primary to secondary deviation can be seen as a major part of the deviant's moral career, although, as we shall have occasion to indicate later on, this career does not necessarily end with the inception of secondary deviation. Generally speaking, a deviant's career is characterized by interaction with agents of social control, other members of the conventional community, and other deviants.

With respect to interaction with agents of social control, the deviant finds himself moving, quite possibly more than once, through certain degrading ceremonies beginning with the act of discovery and culminating in his final placement. One of these stages, the judgment stage, constitutes the labeling or stigmatization phase of the deviant career. Since we can hardly respond to something we do not yet recognize, this process necessarily precedes the larger societal reaction.[39] This latter process is extremely complex, varying along such

lines as social class, religion, kind of deviance under consideration, degree of rejection of the form of deviance, and
cultural differences.

A number of factors also influence the deviant's fate
at the discovery, confrontation, and judgment stages. The
reactions of officials in charge of dealing with apprehended
deviants is one large category of such factors. These officials
have a considerable range of discretion which, when exer-
cised, can be to the deviant's advantage or disadvantage.

Once labeled and publicly known, the deviant ordinarily interacts with a portion of the conventional members
of the community. It can be hypothesized that the longer the
deviant career and the more publicly known and seriously
regarded the deviant acts are, the more difficult it is to
reenter the world of the "normal." However, several other
variables are seen as qualifying this proposition. Whatever
one's chances of success of reentry, these chances are always
mitigated by the general potency of one's deviant status,
which is seen as preeminent over all the person's other identities. Finally, his chances are not facilitated by the incon-
spicuous way in which our society announces that a particular erstwhile deviant has done penance and is now
eligible for readmission to conventional life.

No success or a subjectively perceived low probability of
success by the deviant often leads to further (or possibly
initial) interaction with other deviants. Here, if the individual has not already been so instructed, he soon learns valuable tips for coping with the problems he inevitably
encounters as a deviant. He is also subjected to conformity
pressures since deviant collectivities, like their counterparts
in the conventional world, have their orders of merit and
rules of behavior to which all are expected to show allegi-

ance. Some deviants, however, prefer to eschew unconventional associations either because they are endeavoring to return to the "normal" world or because their behavior can be carried out best in isolation from others (or at least from deviant others).

It is no doubt evident to the reader by now that much of importance to a theoretical discussion of deviance has been omitted. This has been intentional. The theory which we are developing here is concerned with the continuation of deviance and not those factors which figure in its origination. Generally speaking, factors like the strain between cultural and social structures, the generality of cultural norms, and the functionality of deviance continue their influence on subsequent behavior, but in a more or less constant way for the individual. That is to say, these factors do undergo change, but it is change which is gradual and extended over so long a period of time as to go unnoticed by single deviants. On the other hand, the factors discussed in this chapter and the following one are new forces developing out of the fact of one's deviance and working to enhance it or hinder it. In short, we are interested in certain phases of the deviant's career and not those processes and events leading up to it.

The reader will also notice a conspicuous absence of any discussion about a definition of deviance and about norms, the violation of which heralds a deviant act. This is only because we have nothing new to add to the already extensive discussion of these issues, a discussion which seems not to have taken us very far:

> One of the earliest problems the sociologist encounters in his search for a meaningful approach to deviant behavior is that the subject itself does not seem to have any natural

boundaries. Like people in any field, sociologists find it convenient to assume that the deviant person is somehow "different" from those of his fellows who manage to conform, but years of research into the problem have not yielded any important evidence as to what, if anything, this difference might be.[40]

We shall accept as our working definition of deviant behavior that which is defined as such by the community as a whole or its dominant segment.[41] For our purposes this will include all behavior which can be said to be in violation of the moral expectations or norms of the group and for which the individuals concerned are popularly held to be responsible. Criminal property offenses of most kinds fall within this category as do nudism, political radicalism, bohemianism, homosexuality, chronic alcoholism, and religious extremism. Functional mental illness is also included under our rubric of deviance. Following Goffman, Scheff, and others, it can be said to be manifested in the violation of situational norms or the expectations associated with social interaction among men.[42] Although these norms are usually nonmoral ones in the sense that they do not focus on issues of right or wrong, "residual rule-breaking" or "situational improprieties" bring on the label of deviance because such expectations are part of the taken-for-granted world of most members of the community.

Excluded from our definition of deviance and hence from discussion in this book are the behavior and characteristics of constitutionally stigmatized individuals: the blind, the crippled, the deaf, the mentally deficient, the disfigured, and so forth. Although such people may be avoided in many conventional settings, they have not, at least in their physical or mental makeup, violated any community expectations. As a rule we do not expect all men to be able to see, or to hear, or to be without physical deformities; nor do we impute a responsibility to them for their condition when we come upon those so afflicted. Our reason for avoiding them, it may be hypothesized, is not due to their so-called deviance but is related to the difficulties of interaction generated by a lack of common interests and by our inability to cope with the stigmatized characteristic and its effect upon the setting.

NOTES

1. Edwin M. Lemert, *Social Pathology,* pp. 20–21.

2. Ibid., p. 22.

3. Edwin M. Lemert, *Human Deviance, Social Problems, and Social Control,* pp. 41–42.

4. Lemert, *Social Pathology,* pp. 22–23.

5. Ibid., p. 75.

6. Lemert, *Human Deviance, Social Problems, and Social Control,* p. 40.

7. Ibid., pp. 40–41.

8. Lemert, *Social Pathology,* p. 77.

9. Howard S. Becker, *Outsiders: Studies in the Sociology of Deviance,* p. 24.

10. Lemert, *Human Deviance, Social Problems, and Social Control,* p. 40.

11. Becker, *Outsiders,* p. 23. Becker actually speaks about types of deviant behavior rather than types of deviants.

12. Albert K. Cohen, "The Sociology of the Deviant Act," *American Sociological Review* 30 (February 1965): 10.

13. Gregory Bateson, "Bali: The Value System of a Steady

State," in *Social Structure: Studies Presented to A. R. Radcliffe-Brown,* ed. Meyer Fortes, pp. 36–39.

14. The stages of confrontation, judgment, and placement were originally developed by Parsons in the *The Social System* for application to medical patients. Erikson has recently recast them into a general deviance framework. See Kai Erikson, "Notes on the Sociology of Deviance," in *The Other Side,* ed. Howard S. Becker, p. 16.

15. Harold Garfinkle, "Conditions of Successful Degradation Ceremonies," *American Journal of Sociology* 61 (March 1956): 420. A situation that augments this change in self-conception is the tendency for the conventional part of the community to interpret all past, present, and prospective behavior in terms of the new status (ibid., p. 422).

16. Jerome H. Skolnick, *Justice Without Trial,* passim. DeLamater has recently discussed deviance in a framework similar to the one which is being developed in this chapter. However, there are a number of important differences between our formulation and his, one of which should be noted here since it concerns labeling. He seems to limit this procedure to the formal agencies in the community, whereas we have recognized that this function may not only take place informally among ordinary citizens as well as among officials, but also that unofficial stigmatization, whatever its source, may influence the formal processes. See John DeLamater, "On the Nature of Deviance," *Social Forces* 46 (Fall 1968): 445–455.

17. It is being suggested here that his contact with the agents of judgment is itself a stigmatizing event in some cases which can lead to treatment not unlike that experienced by publicly labeled deviants. See Richard D. Schwartz and Jerome H. Skolnick, "Two Studies of Legal Stigma," in *The Other Side,* ed. Becker, pp. 108–109.

18. Albert K. Cohen, "The Study of Social Disorganization and Deviant Behavior," in *Sociology Today: Problems and Prospects,* ed. Robert K. Merton, Leonard Broom, and Leonard S. Cottrell, Jr., p. 465, n. 4. Merton's types of adaptation may be

found in Robert K. Merton, *Social Theory and Social Structure,* rev. ed., pp. 139–157.

19. Becker, *Outsiders,* pp. 34–35.

20. See, for example, Irving Piliavin and Scott Briar, "Police Encounters with Juveniles," *American Journal of Sociology* 70 (September 1964): 206–214; Egon Bittner, "The Police on Skid-Row," *American Sociological Review* 32 (October 1967): 699–715.

21. See, for example, John I. Kitsuse, "Societal Reaction to Deviant Behavior," in *The Other Side,* ed. Becker, pp. 87–102; Derek L. Phillips, "Education, Psychiatric Sophistication, and the Rejection of Mentally Ill Help-Seekers," *The Sociological Quarterly* 8 (Winter 1967): 122–132; Elizabeth A. Rooney and Don C. Gibbons, "Social Reactions to 'Crimes Without Victims,'" *Social Problems* 13 (Spring 1966): 400–410; Bruce P. Dohrenwend and Edwin Chin–Shong, "Social Status and Attitudes Toward Psychological Disorder," *American Sociological Review* 32 (June 1967): 417–433. For a generalized discussion of other variables in the societal reaction, see Lemert, *Social Pathology,* pp. 52, 62–63, 98; and idem, *Human Deviance, Social Problems, and Social Control,* p. 49.

22. Kai T. Erikson, *Wayward Puritans,* chap. 3.

23. See, for example, Lemert's work on stuttering among the Pacific Coastal Indians and certain Polynesian groups. Lemert, *Human Deviance, Social Problems, and Social Control,* pp. 138, 148–151.

24. Talcott Parsons, *The Social System,* p. 175.

25. Becker, *Outsiders,* pp. 34–35.

26. If this can happen to the acquitted-suspected deviant, it certainly can happen to those returning to conventional life after being labeled and punished for a deviant act.

27. This is essentially what Glaser concluded after his large-scale survey of federal ex-offenders in the United States. Daniel Glaser, *The Effectiveness of a Prison and Parole System,* p. 473.

28. Harold Sampson, et al., "The Mental Hospital and Marital Family Ties," in *The Other Side,* ed. Becker, pp. 139–162.

29. Schwartz and Skolnick, "Two Studies of Legal Stigma," in *The Other Side,* ed. Becker, pp. 103–116. This was found to hold for medical doctors accused of malpractice.

30. Erikson, "Notes on the Sociology of Deviance," pp. 16–17.

31. See, for example, Marsh B. Ray, "The Cycle of Abstinence and Relapse Among Heroin Addicts," in *The Other Side,* ed. Becker, pp. 173–175.

32. This includes most categories of deviants as long as they carry on their activities collectively. Among juvenile delinquents, this manifests itself as "techniques of neutralization." See David Matza, *Delinquency and Drift,* pp. 60–62. For evidence of this phenomenon among jazz musicians, see Howard S. Becker, "The Professional Dance Musician and His Audience," *American Journal of Sociology* 57 (September 1951): 136–144; Robert A. Stebbins, "The Conflict Between Musical and Commercial Values in the Minneapolis Jazz Community," *Proceedings of the Minnesota Academy of Science* 30 (1962): 75–79. Becker provides for such ideological activities among marihuana smokers in Howard S. Becker, "Marihuana Use and Social Control," in *Human Behavior and Social Processes,* ed. Arnold M. Rose, pp. 589–607. For Beats, see Ned Polsky, *Hustlers, Beats, and Others,* pp. 169–172. Homophile organizations like The Mattachine Society and One, Inc. and their associated publications can be seen as supporting evidence for a similar phenomenon among homosexuals. One major exception to this apparently general rule that deviants who interact a great deal among themselves produce collective rationalizations for their antisocial behavior is the poolroom hustler. See ibid., p. 65.

33. Howard S. Becker, "History, Culture and Subjective Experience: An Exploration of the Social Bases of Drug-Induced Experiences," *Journal of Health and Social Behavior* 8 (September 1967): 163–176.

34. David Krech, Richard S. Crutchfield, and Egerton L. Ballachey, *Individual in Society,* p. 529.

35. Ibid., pp. 512–515.

36. Erving Goffman, *Stigma: Notes on the Management of Spoiled Identity,* pp. 143–144.

37. See, for example, Glaser, *Effectiveness of Prison and Parole,* p. 391. He says "Our interviews suggest that most ex-prisoners strive to dissociate themselves from their former colleagues and to disengage themselves from prison ties."

38. The recent origination of the reportedly viable Schizophrenics Anonymous International in Saskatoon, Saskatchewan, in addition to other such organizations, indicates that only some of the mentally ill remain alone. See *The Evening Telegram* (St. John's, Newfoundland), 13 September 1967, p. 35; also Henry Wechsler, "The Ex-patient Organization," *Journal of Social Issues* 16 (1960): 47–53; David Landy and Sara E. Singer, "The Social Organization and Culture of a Club for Former Mental Patients," *Human Relations* 14 (February 1961): 31–41.

39. This notion appears to underlie one of Scheff's causal hypotheses of mental illness: "among residual rule-breakers, labeling is the single most important cause of careers of residual deviance." See Thomas J. Scheff, *Being Mentally Ill,* pp. 92–93.

40. Erikson, *Wayward Puritans,* p. 5.

41. For a discussion of the definition of deviance, see Lemert, *Social Pathology,* pp. 30–50; Leslie T. Wilkins, *Social Deviance: Social Policy, Action, and Research,* chap. 4.

42. See Erving Goffman, *Behavior in Public Places,* chap. 14; idem, *Interaction Ritual,* pp. 137–148; Thomas J. Scheff, *Being Mentally Ill,* chap. 2. A list of several studies bearing on this theme can be found in Michael Argyle and Adam Kendon, "The Experimental Analysis of Social Performance," in *Advances in Experimental Social Psychology,* ed. Leonard Berkowitz, 3:88–90. Cahnman has recently written about obesity as residual deviance which can be placed under the heading of the violation of "physical appearance" rules in the Argyle and Kendon framework. See Werner J. Cahnman, "The Stigma of Obesity," *The Sociological Quarterly* 9 (Summer 1968): 283–299.

2

COMMITMENT AS A CAREER CONTINGENCY

We have assessed the current literature in light of the concept of the deviant career, to bring us to the point where we can begin to modify and add to it. First, however, it seems necessary to present an adequate defense of this usage of the term career as a result of some recent remarks by Lemert. He has reservations about the utility of this idea in studying deviance:

> Closer examination of the career concept suggests that its application to deviance should be guarded. I doubt, for example, that the notion of "recruitment" of persons to most kinds of deviance can be any more than a broad analogy. . . . A career denotes a course to be run, but the delineation of fixed sequences or stages through which persons move from less to more serious deviance is difficult or impossible to reconcile with an interactional theory. Furthermore, no incontrovertible evidence has yet been marshaled to justify the belief that prodromal signs of deviance exist.[1]

In stating the case for the idea of the deviant career, it is helpful if we emphasize and sharpen the distinction between career pattern and career. According to Nosow and Form a career pattern is "any pattern of occupational change (vertical and/or horizontal) of any occupational group."[2] This essentially cultural phenomenon can be contrasted with the individual-objective notion of career as presented by Becker: a career is a "patterned series of adjustments made by the individual to the network of institutions, formal organizations, and informal relationships in which the work of the occupation is performed."[3] Here the sociologist's point of view is emphasized.

There is still a third way to approach the phenomenon of career: it can be viewed subjectively, as a personally real concept in an individual's mind. Goffman touches on this distinction in the passage below:

> One value of the concept of career is its two-sidedness. One side is linked to internal matters held dearly and closely, such as image of self and felt identity; the other side concerns official position, jural relations, and style of life, and is part of a publicly accessible institutional complex.[4]

This perspective, though yet undeveloped, emphasizes the actor's recognition and interpretation of past events in his biography and especially his interpretation of the various important contingencies as they are encountered. More specifically, career in this sense is the person's awareness of a past sequence of events associated with a particular identity deemed significant by one or more of his reference groups, a sequence which is usually seen as extending into the future with some degree of clarity. The importance of recognition and interpretation of past events plus its connection with a specific social identity distinguish the subjective career from the kindred idea of personal history or biography.

When career patterns do not exist with any degree of clarity, as in many forms of deviance, then the subjective career is apparent mostly in retrospect. Thus, many deviants, especially those who find their identity to be degrading, discover that their moral behavior does have a certain recognizable order when they pause to cast a backward glance. Of course, a career in this sense is not apparent at all until the actor has participated in his special way of life long enough to be able to discern a pattern in his own history, perhaps aided by observations made on the histories of his fellow deviants. How much prospective recognition of a career there is depends upon the kind of deviance being considered; presumably a definable course to be traveled is best developed in those forms to which their adherents are positively attached.[5]

When these conceptualizations are recast into a deviance framework, we can see that there is not enough knowledge about the fate of various groups of deviants to warrant a discussion of career patterns; and if Lemert's criticisms may be understood in this sense, then he is correct. Career in the subjective sense is most compatible with our conceptualization of commitment, and this usage will be employed throughout this study. An ambitious program of research should in time provide us with the knowledge necessary to talk meaningfully about career patterns, including even recruitment in some kinds of deviance.[6]

There is another possible misunderstanding about the idea of deviant career which must be dealt with before we can go on: namely, how long does it last? We are hardly prepared to give specific lengths of deviant careers at this stage of inquiry, if indeed we will ever be, but it is obvious, both theoretically and empirically, that the career of any single deviant does not inevitably culminate in secondary deviance. As they have been presented in the last chapter, the associated career contingencies enhance or hinder progress toward continued deviance; they are turning points which push a person out of deviance into marginal or even conventional surroundings or which further draw him in. There is no reason, given a sufficient amount of research, why kinds of career contingencies could not have as much predictive value as most other social science propositions. In short, the career of a deviant is his perception of his passage through turning points which may lead to a career in the conventional world or to an extended deviant career. It does not necessarily go on forever.[7]

In fact one might say that when the deviant passes to a marginal or conventional identity (and does not return to deviance), he is beginning a "second career": a career now centered around an occupation or job of some sort.[8] This applies, of course, only to those deviants who are not legitimately employed. Other deviants simply end their deviant careers. Later in this chapter we shall discuss these points more thoroughly.

Perhaps this indeterminacy of the length of the deviant career is nowhere more exposed than in the phases where the person has been publicly labeled and with this stigma attempts to interact with conventional members of the community and also possibly with other deviants. It is this set of career contingencies which is the focus of this book. The theory of commitment outlined below is offered as a way

of organizing the disparate notions which have been introduced in recent years about the destiny of publicly known
deviants.

COMMITMENT: A THEORY
OF FORCED BEHAVIOR[9]

It is possible to isolate at least three different meanings of
the term commitment, all of which enjoy some degree of
currency among contemporary social scientists. For instance, Webster's Dictionary defines it as "the act of committing to charge, keeping, or trust" in one sense of the
word, and this is the meaning familiar to those who engage
in the practices of hospitalization and incarceration. On the
other hand, sociologists and psychologists have for a long
time discussed value commitment or some equivalent form
which involves a positive personal attraction to a cognitive
state, an attraction ordinarily accompanied by a favorable
self-image. It appears that much of the work on commitment
to attitudes which has been carried out in experimental social psychology is concerned with this kind of commitment.[10]

A third meaning of commitment is phrased in the dictionary as the pledge to carry out or support some action or
idea. It is the extension of this sense of the word which is of
interest to us here, an extension that originated in occupational sociology and the study of deviance.[11] This form of
commitment, called "continuance commitment" by Kanter,
refers to the fact that people engage in consistent lines of

behavior because they are threatened by certain penalties for not doing so. It is characteristic of commitment, in this usage, that the actor rejects certain alternatives, and that the behavior associated with the identity or expectation to which one is committed persists over time.[12] Based upon these observations and others to follow we can more formally define this idea as *the awareness of the impossibility of choosing a different social identity or rejecting a particular expectation because of the imminence of penalties involved in making the switch.*[13]

According to Abramson, the penalties involved in commitment of this kind can be many and varied:

> Committed lines . . . are sequences of action with penalties and costs so arranged as to guarantee their selection. Penalty may be informal or formal. It may be externally or internally administered. Penalty may range from the pangs of conscience to criminal prosecution. The penalty, whatever its nature, is brought to bear on the actor for any action other than the one recognized as legitimate. The legitimacy of action lies in previous commitment or inner compulsion to follow only certain lines of action.[14]

Commitment is also something that people are aware of. It is possible that at the inception of the urge to adopt a particular identity or enact a particular form of behavior one may be unaware of the future implications, but sooner or later, when he tries to abandon that identity or expectation, he becomes conscious of the consequences or penalties that accompany deviation from the legitimate line.

This is congruent with Goffman's view of commitment. He further suggests that the term commitment refer to those cases where the person is forced to adhere to a specified line

of action. "Attachment," however, is not a forced condition. An individual becomes attached to a line of behavior
when "the self-image available for anyone entering a particular position is one of which he may become affectively
and cognitively enamored, desiring and expecting to see
himself in terms of the enactment of the role and the self-
identification emerging from this enactment." [15] Attachment
is very similar to, if not identical with, the commitment to
values spoken of earlier. However, Goffman also notes that
commitment and attachment can occur together, a point which
is especially pertinent for our purposes.

We are concerned in this study with commitment to a
social identity or to an expectation of behavior as Goffman,
Becker, Abramson, and Kanter have used this term. Our
aim is to present the rudiments of a theory of continuance
commitment of broad enough scope to be of interest to social
scientists and practitioners in general as well as to those
specifically concerned with deviance. It is also hoped that
this framework will be complete enough to serve as a guide
to future research. However, because of the roots of this view
of commitment in areas of occupations and deviance, our illustrations will, of necessity, be drawn from them.[16]

THE PRECONDITIONS
OF COMMITMENT

One of the weaknesses of the past discussions of continuance
commitment is the lack of clarity of this central concept. As
a first step toward a coherent theory, we shall attempt to de-

fine further what is meant by commitment and what the preconditions are for its appearance. Before commitment can be said to be established, the following preconditions must first be present: (1) there must be arrangements which can produce penalties; (2) the penalties must in fact be produced; (3) these penalties are perceived as imminent; (4) the committed individual is aware of his state; (5) there are objectively possible alternatives to the committed identity or expectation. These are presented below in greater detail.

Penalty-producing Arrangements

Commitment, as we have just pointed out, can be to an identity or to a single expectation of behavior. As Howard Becker has observed, certain arrangements in our daily lives work to foster this commitment by producing penalties.[17]

Even though we do not intend to present an exhaustive list, it will facilitate our aims if we cast the welter of penalty-producing arrangements in society into a twofold classification based upon their relationship to a specific social identity or to a specific expectation. The first kind, which we shall call *identity-committing arrangements,* is founded on the idea that by means of certain events or conditions one becomes committed to a particular social identity and its associated configuration of expectations of behavior.[18] A number of examples can be cited.

Thus, legal contracts can commit us to specific identities, as in the legal basis of marriage and divorce or in that of naturalized citizenship. Becker has noted that impersonal bureaucratic arrangements, such as pension funds and seniority, constrain a person from shifting his occupational identity. He has also observed that adjustments to new positions or identities may eventuate in commitment. Such adjustments come to be so much a part of the individual that he unfits himself for any other identity or position. In all these cases the individual in question has become committed to certain identities.

Everett Hughes has recognized that ceremonies commit us.[19] Ceremonies that mark status passages (and we might add, their associated symbols), such as a wedding, a graduation, or an inauguration, publicly announce the new identity in a manner difficult to deny. In an analogous fashion the judgment phase in a deviant's moral career, discussed in Chapter 1, announces a new identity for the person concerned which helps commit him to that identity.

In connection with deviance, and perhaps other identities as well, it may be noted that certain physiological arrangements can produce commitment. Probably the best-known example is that of the narcotics addict whose body equilibrium is painfully upset when he does not satisfy his craving for the drug:

> The continuousness of the craving for drugs in human subjects is clearly connected with human beings' capacity to anticipate the future and hence to obtain supplies to forestall future distress, and also with the ability to remember and reconstruct the past so as to understand that the withdrawal distress of the present is connected with a long series of events in the past and with bodily changes induced by those events.[20]

One may also commit himself by presenting a certain characterization or image of himself to others in the social situation, thereby planting the expectation that he will be that kind of person under the same circumstances in the future.[21] The person who has excelled as a wit at a party may well be expected to adopt that same identity at the next one, providing those at the second gathering have observed him or heard about him in this capacity.

Finally, one often commits himself by investing great amounts of time, energy, and money in some enterprise or identity. Thus the businessman who spends thousands of dollars and thousands of hours developing a corner grocery store is in no position, as a rule, to quit to take up medicine. Conversely, the physician who has invested as much in getting an education is not prepared to drop everything to go into the grocery business. A closely related arrangement is the renunciation of investments already made, as in the case of the disposal of earthly possessions in response to religious beliefs.[22]

The preceding illustrations of the identity-committing arrangement can be contrasted with those exemplifying the *expectation-committing arrangement*. The latter refers to the fact that by the force of certain circumstances people do get committed to one or a few expectations of behavior that pertain only to specific categories of social situations, situations which may or may not be recurrent. Usually such expectations are part of a larger configuration of expectations associated with some social identity. However, unlike identity-committing arrangements they do not commit one to that total configuration by being committed to the associated identity.

One of the best-known examples of expectation-committing arrangements is to be found in the body of experimental investigations growing out of the work of Kurt

Lewin. Here it has been found that public announcement of an intended behavior is more likely to result in that behavior actually being carried out than if the intention is not made public.[23] Most of these studies have dealt with intentions to do a particular thing, such as eat sweetbreads during World War II, rather than with intentions to become a certain person (that is, to change social identities).

It seems that the usage of the term "decision" by Festinger and others permits us to classify it much of the time as an expectation-committing arrangement. Festinger states "that a decision carries commitment with it if the decision unequivocally affects subsequent behavior. This is not to mean that the decision is irrevocable, but rather that the decision has clear implications for the subsequent unrolling of events as long as the person stays with that decision." [24] The important element here is the cognitive state of having made a decision rather than, as in the last paragraph, having made public that decision or some other claim.

Presumably legal contracts and other similar arrangements can also lead to commitment to one or a few expectations. For example, a musician is contracted to give a performance for one night at a local concert hall or a person is required to appear in court as a result of a traffic ticket. Howard Becker has observed that a particular expectation from the general body of cultural expectations carries with it penalties for nonobservance.[25] Rules of etiquette can be viewed from this standpoint.

Edward Jones has noticed that attempts at ingratiation can commit us to specific actions in the future:

> In forecasting the most likely effects of his own behavior, the would-be ingratiator must realize that the acceptance

of a complimentary evaluation is a function both of the criteria on which it seems to be based and of the extent to which the evaluation involves a commitment to present or future actions.[26]

As far as deviant behavior is concerned, our interests center on arrangements that commit one to an identity. It is not denied that deviants, like most other people, become committed to single expectations; in fact, these arrangements may someday be found to play a significant role in explaining deviant behavior. Nevertheless, in this study we shall focus entirely on identity-committing arrangements, so as to keep our project within manageable limits.

The Penalties

We can distinguish three kinds of penalties: psychological, biological, and social. Social penalties originate in the actions of other people and are experienced by a committed person because he has opened himself to their influence. These people, it should be noted, can be those role-others associated with the committed identity or expectation, or they can be people associated with an identity to which the actor would like to switch. He can also experience penalties from both sides during certain periods of his life. Thus, a low opportunity for legitimate work because of his criminal record is a penalty that the reforming ex-offender experiences in the nondeviant world,[27] while in the criminal world he may experience the penalty of a constant threat to life and limb for violation of certain subcultural norms.

Psychological penalties originate in the mental strain created by attempts to abandon a committed identity, such as in the stress one undergoes when giving up a strongly held ideology. Biological penalties stem from a physico-physiological condition of the person which develops when he tries to move to a different way of life. Here, too, there may be penalties in whatever he does, as in the case of withdrawal symptoms accrued from attempts at renunciation of narcotics versus the social penalties of stigma and imprisonment acquired for maintaining such an identity.

Since it is now evident that, whatever one does with respect to his committed state, penalties exist, it will facilitate future discussion if we classify these. Hence, we shall refer to those penalties, social, physiological, or psychological, which arise when one attempts to leave a committed identity or expectation as *renunciation penalties.* We shall label as *continuation penalties* those costs endured, regardless of what kind they are, when the person remains in the identity or expectation to which he is committed. By phrasing the matter in this fashion, there is no need, given the explanatory aims of a theory of forced behavior (continuance commitment), to be concerned with rewards.[28]

The combination of these various classes of penalties yields the following types:

	Renunciation penalties	Continuation penalties
Social penalties	Renunciation social penalties	Continuation social penalties
Psychological penalties	Renunciation psychological penalties	Continuation psychological penalties
Biological penalties	Renunciation biological penalties	Continuation biological penalties

The Imminence of Penalties

For commitment to occur, these penalties must be recognized as real and imminent by the individual affected by them. They are not abstract possibilities realizable in the dim future, but poignant threats to one's well-being ready to strike should one behave the wrong way. Penalties are most imminent when they exist in an easily accessible or actually existing social situation; when it is readily apparent to the actor that if he acts in this particular way, a particular undesirable event is likely to take place. They are also imminent when they are recognized as having a high probability of occurrence at some future date. Thus, the Chicago public school teacher who works in the slums clearly recognizes that after learning new teaching and disciplinary techniques, learning the appropriate expectations with regard to student performance, and acquiring an understanding of her pupils, she will suffer the imminent social and psychological penalties of finding these adjustments unsatisfactory if she should decide to move to a middle-class school.[29]

Awareness of Commitment

The actor becomes aware of commitment when he becomes aware of the real and imminent penalties facing him if he attempts to renounce a specific identity or expectation. As such it is a subjective state, an "acquired behavioral disposition," [30] which has developed gradually from the accumulated retrospective and prospective definitions or interpretations of events in one's past and anticipated social and physical surroundings.[31] Thus, the study of commitment concentrates on the actor's point of view and not on that of the observer.

Events which are seen as penalizing and therefore committing for one person will not necessarily be perceived in this way by another.

The nonprofessional criminals interviewed in this study were conscious of the imminence of several kinds of penalties stemming from their interpersonal relations with conventional members of the community. For instance, most of them disliked and tried to avoid situations where others present, who were unaware of their deviant identity, discussed criminals pejoratively. The professionals, on the other hand, showed noticeably less distaste for such interchanges; they admitted often taking issue with the remarks made by "squares" in an attempt to enlighten their thinking.

Alternatives and Penalties

All of what we have said so far in this section presupposes an observation made earlier: alternatives are available. It is objectively possible to renounce the identity or expectation to which one is committed; one has a choice in selecting what he considers to be the least costly alternative. Usually this first involves a more or less conscious subjective weighing of the penalties associated with each alternative. Whichever alternative carries the most favorable or preferable balance is then chosen; this, as we postulated in Chapter 1, is a function of the structure of personality.[32] It is possible, of course, to have any combination of social, psychological, or biological penalties associated with any alternative. This process of weighing penalties is evident in Finestone's investigation of the recidivism of Polish offenders, which revealed that the costs of inadequate performance in family and work roles by the released prisoner tipped the balance of penalties in favor of further deviance. Inadequate performances led to

> an awareness of the extremely limited nature of their pros-
> pects of becoming reinstated in non-deviant roles, and
> to . . . the reorientation of their behavior around a new
> view of themselves as disillusioned, baffled, and defeated
> men. Such a sense of defeat tended to initiate a process of
> personal demoralization, frequently accompanied by exces-
> sive drinking, and by their progressive withdrawal from
> their already attenuated conventional ties. They now had
> little choice but to consort with others of similar back-
> ground. Nevertheless, it is important to recognize that they
> could do so without intent of reverting to criminality and
> solely out of a wish for acceptance. Once such ties were
> formed, however, contingencies were likely to arise in
> which they were subject to procriminal pressures.[33]

The psychological state of commitment presupposes that the choice of alternatives is a relatively easy one for the individual concerned; namely, that there is a subjectively large preferability gap, as seen in the balance of penalties, beween the alternative to which he is committed (more desirable) and the one which he has rejected (less desirable). Obviously, a roughly equal balance of penalties will produce a certain amount of vacillation between alternative identities or expectations—what is traditionally known as role-conflict.

It should be noted, in passing, that certain identities present no choice at all. Because of their immutable biological roots, identities like sex, height, mental deficiency, and constitutionally based forms of mental illness deny us any alternative.[34] People in such categories cannot abandon their identity, no matter what the penalties, and our theory of commitment will not be applied here. It does not help to explain the persistence of the behavior of people in these kinds of identities. It is an essential condition of commitment that an objective choice be available.

THE STATE OF COMMITMENT

It should be noted that being committed does not prevent one from interacting with those outside the circle of people associated with the committed identity or committed expectation. Nor does it restrain one from doing some of those things bound to bring on certain psychological or biological penalties. All it prevents is a *total* rejection of the committed identity or expectation for a different but more penalizing one. People are able to endure some of the costs of deviating from a committed state, but not enough of them to make a true break with it. This, of course, depends upon the nature of the penalties and their subjective interpretation.

Furthermore, being committed to one identity involves only part, really a small part, of any person's total repertoire of activities. Much of the time the individual is enacting role expectations associated with other identities, although in the case of deviance we have indicated that these other identities may come to be at least partly overshadowed by the deviant one. Much hinges upon the visibility of the stigmatizing characteristics.

We must be careful that a scientific statement of commitment to identities does not lead us to overemphasize the fact that behavior is restricted. Continuance commitment is a cognitive state which makes it unlikely that one will renounce a specific identity or expectation of behavior, but it does not completely prevent interaction with others (except to some extent for deviants) in the noncommitted spheres of life, nor does it even prevent some flirtation with the various penalties. There are other qualifications to be made on the state of commitment which will be presented further on in this chapter, under the heading, "Limits of Commitment."

COMMITMENT AND DEVIANCE

We have already indicated that for this study the theory of commitment is intended to organize the disparate notions and facts associated with the interaction of the publicly known deviant with other deviants and with the conventional members of the community. This is one part of the process of individuation of deviance about which we know little. Yet it is a critical part, since it is in this phase of the deviant's career that he makes the transition from primary to secondary deviation.

From the discussion in the last section, it is now possible to see how and under what circumstances the committed deviant feels compelled to remain in his identity. But what about Goffman's distinction between attachment and commitment presented earlier in this chapter? Does the idea of attachment have any import for the study of deviance? If so, how does it relate to commitment as we have developed the idea here and to the notion of the deviant career? We shall deal with these questions below.

Attachment and Commitment

It is implied by Goffman that people who are attached to
certain lines of behavior are not forced to hold such a position.
They are engaging in such behavior because it appeals to
them, and because it enhances their self-images. Yet, he
does mention that attachment can occur with commitment,
and this is the point which is relevant for the study of deviance, and one which needs further interpretation. For it seems
that attachment to a deviant line of behavior, if it endures
until one becomes publicly recognized for such activities, always involves commitment, an issue to be taken up shortly.

Commitment accompanying attachment to a line of behavior is produced from at least two sets of penalties. The
first of these is the same set of social penalties which operates
under the conditions of unattached commitment: the pressures
emanating from the wider community as manifested in ridicule and other informal and formal means of social control.
It is hypothesized here that a deviant in this position knows
quite well how the wider community feels about him; and,
even though he does not intend to abandon his way of life,
he is, to a greater or lesser extent, aware of the restrictions
to association outside his own circle. Under these circumstances attachment is accompanied by commitment only when
the community knows of his past or present activities or
the deviant thinks it knows.

The second set of penalties refers to the interpersonal
and psychological consequences encountered when one tries
to abandon a powerful and long-standing ideological position. Often one will have accumulated no small number of
friends who, unless they are also changing their beliefs, will
create tension for the individual by trying to retain him in

their circle. Moreover, evidence from an investigation of radical political beliefs suggests that the amount of inner conflict generated by switching value orientations is extensive.[35] Perhaps this is due, in part, to the fact that to give up a value orientation in which one is highly ego-involved is to give up part of one's self. To be attached is to be committed to one's own personality.[36] Of course, these interpersonal and psychological penalties are also encountered when one switches from one strongly held conventional value orientation to another; although because of the lack of the deviant element, they are probably less severe.

It can be seen from what has been said so far that there are actually two genres of continuance commitment in deviance: that which involves attachment and that which does not. It would be valuable if this distinction were reflected in our theoretical terminology. Therefore we propose discarding the term attachment and retaining the idea of self-image which apparently underlies Goffman's distinction. From here on commitment based on attachment to deviant values will be referred to as *self-enhancing commitment,* and commitment based on factors other than such attachment will be called *self-degrading commitment.*[37]

A note of caution about this distinction is in order before we move on to a discussion of commitment and the deviant career. The adjectives self-enhancing and self-degrading refer only to the extent to which the actor either finds something in the identity which he is proud of, something which supports a positive self-identification, or the opposite, something which produces a negative self-image for him. However, there will always be other aspects of any social identity (be it attractive or unattractive) more or less independent of self-image considerations, aspects which in themselves are attractive or unattractive. For example, the nonprofessional criminal who is committed to his identity in a self-degrading way may still enjoy certain benefits from that way of life which make the identity and its behavioral configuration attractive to him; benefits such as freedom from the rigid hours of legitimate employment or the intense excitement of the "caper."

In short, the self-enhancing value of an identity is to be considered a reward and the self-degrading value a penalty. A positive self-image in an identity may function as a significant reward, outweighing many penalties in the balance; but even this reward can at times be outweighed, as in the case of the respectable citizen of the community whose personal problems are so penalizing that even the degrading status of an alcoholic is preferred.

Self-enhancing Commitment and the Deviant Career

Daniel Glaser has already described the processes of socialization and internalization by which the deviant (specifically, the criminal deviant) comes to be committed in a self-enhancing way.[38] All that remains for us to do is to place this kind of commitment in the framework of the deviant career.

Since commitment to any identity involves a recognition of imminent penalties that will materialize if that identity is abandoned, self-enhancing commitment must occur at some later point. It would therefore seem that this type of commitment could be located at certain specific stages in the deviant's career: (1) wherever the individual becomes aware of the interpersonal and psychological renunciation penalties (the commitment to self and commitment to associates men-

tioned earlier) restraining him from abandoning his disgrace-
ful identity, (2) when he becomes aware of the renunciation
penalties incurred from the outside conventional world for
his deviant activities. Of course, costs could be experienced
only after one or more judgment phases of the deviant career,
since the deviant must first be known to the community. An
individual could very easily experience both kinds of penalties, and either could occur first in his career.

With respect to the kinds of penalties that commit one
to an identity, it is assumed that the subject is aware of at
least some of these beforehand. For instance, a person knows
that his associates will oppose his leaving their company,
knowledge which is probably gained from watching how
they treat others who attempt to do so. Most of us, at one
time or another, have probably recognized the importance of
certain identities to our own self-conception, especially when
we have considered abandoning them or have felt them
threatened. The same knowledge is being assumed for the
deviant who is committed in a self-enhancing way to a deviant
identity. Because the individual deviant has grown up with
some contact with conventional society, he has an idea of
how its members feel about people of his kind. Thus, the
deviant person can anticipate these penalties on the basis of
prior knowledge without actually having to leave his identity.

Some of these themes are evident in Chic Conwell's
comments as he portrays the view of the professional thief:

> Other thieves leave the institution with the determination
> not to resume the racket. But as soon as they get out they
> meet trouble. They have ten dollars and a suit of clothes
> which spots them as just out of stir. Unless he has friends,
> he has to begin his career by stealing a suit of clothes. The

job he has promised him if he has come out on parole, which seldom happens for professional thieves, is generally phony. No one wants to employ a professional thief, and he cannot get a job by his own efforts. . . . A certain thief stated about one month after he had been released from prison: "during the last month I have had at least forty invitations from thieves to go out stealing with them, but I have not had a single suggestion from a legitimate person about how I could make some money honestly." . . . He gets panicky about his ability to get a job; he keeps wondering how long he can last. At the same time he has the confidence in his ability to make plenty of money by stealing. He says to himself: "Why the hell should I starve to death when I can go out and steal all I want? Why live in this lousy place in dirty and patched clothes when I can by stealing get all the comforts of life?" His confidence in his ability is the big thing about his continuing in the racket.[39]

On the basis of what has been said so far, the following are presented as examples of self-enhancing commitment among deviants: engaging in nudism, political radicalism, professional crime, bohemianism, playing jazz (where it is considered deviant),[40] espousing extreme religious values, and quite possibly using marihuana and LSD.

Self-degrading Commitment and the Deviant Career

The case for self-degrading commitment differs slightly but significantly from that of the self-enhancing variety. The major difference, as we have already indicated, is the lack of any genuine enhancement of one's self-image. Thus, the first category of penalties associated with self-enhancing commitment does not apply here since there is, at least initially, little or no desire to be with other like deviants, and little loss of one's positive self-conception if one tries to abandon this identity. The second category of penalties, however—the penalties stemming from interaction with those in the conventional community—is very much a reality, and depends as before upon a sufficient amount of visibility and public labeling for adequate community identification. It may be hypothesized that this same group of penalties may lead even the falsely accused deviant into commitment.

Furthermore, different psychological penalties exist for deviants committed in a self-degrading manner, penalties often, though not necessarily, connected with certain biological costs. Hence, the drug addict who would like to abandon this practice suffers not only withdrawal symptoms but also a certain amount of mental stress, if such stress is what first drove him to seek a solution in narcotics. There is growing evidence that emotional maladjustment under specific conditions leads to some sort of psychosomatic disorder, such as certain gastrointestinal disturbances, high blood pressure, bronchial asthma, and the like.[41] Thus, to the extent that one can avoid these disorders by the use of deviant retreatist methods or some psychological mode of adjustment, they can be seen as biological penalties which accrue when one attempts to abandon these methods.

The location of self-degrading commitment as a contingency in the deviant career appears to be much the same as that of the self-enhancing kind.[42] There are two possible places, depending upon the sort of penalty under consideration: (1) whenever the individual becomes aware of the biological and psychological renunciation penalties which await him if he should abandon his deviant identity, and (2) when he becomes aware of the renunciation penalties acquired from interaction with those in the conventional community. Again, an individual could easily experience both kinds of penalties, and either one could occur before the other in his particular career.

From current knowledge one can say that the following are restrained from abandoning their deviant identity because of the self-degrading nature of their commitment: the homosexual, the compulsive gambler, the chronic alcoholic, the drug addict, the nonprofessional criminal, and the functionally mentally ill.

THE LIMITS OF COMMITMENT

Earlier we defined continuance commitment as the impossibility of choosing a different identity or rejecting a particular expectation because of the imminence of penalties involved in making the change. We emphasized the imminence of these penalties in that the individual is reasonably sure they will take place if he abandons his identity or expectation. Thus, for that person it is subjectively improbable that he will adopt a new status or abandon a given expectation.

No one has systematically studied the barriers to the development of commitment or the limits of its duration. In fact, the literature gives the impression that commitment, once acquired, is extremely difficult, if not impossible, to lose—implying that there are no limits. Yet there is reason to believe that this is a highly variable matter when the many forms of commitment are considered.

In contemplating the barriers to full commitment in deviance, much depends upon the kind of deviance being considered and the nature of the renunciation and continuation penalties associated with it. All forms of deviance have some social penalties or penalties that are imposed upon the individual by members of the wider community or by other deviants; whereas the biological penalties are found only in certain kinds of deviance, such as homosexuality, drug addiction, and some of the mental illnesses. Psychological penalties are like the biological in the sense that they, too, are limited to certain forms of deviance (e.g., religious cultism, political radicalism, chronic alcoholism).

The important characteristic of these different categories of penalties is not that some of them are harder to endure than others (perhaps someday it will be discovered that, in fact, this is true), but that the occurrence of some of them is more *inevitable* than the occurrence of others. Especially the biological and perhaps even the psychological penalties have a high subjective as well as objective probability of occurrence. The social penalties, on the other hand, are much less inevitable. For instance, it has been observed that the societal reaction to deviance varies greatly along social class and religious dimensions even within the same geographical community. It also varies with the kind of deviance; that is, it varies between the seriously regarded and not so seriously regarded forms. For a reaction even to take place a minimum of notoriety and visibility on the part of the deviant is required, which depends among other things upon the number of times he is judged as being such a person and the efficiency of both the formal and informal channels of communication on such matters. From the individual's point of view, it may be easier to choose to bypass, disbelieve, or misunderstand a communication from others about himself than to ignore a physical or even a psychological fact.[43]

Thus, on the basis of one of the oldest principles in the psychology of learning, it can be suggested that because social penalties provide only irregular reinforcement, the subjective knowledge that such penalties are imminent will take much longer to develop, if in fact it ever does. This hypothesis immediately raises the question of which forms of deviance are least likely to bring on psychological and biological renunciation penalties for abandonment and most likely to bring on social renunciation penalties. While there may be others, the one major category of deviance that comes to mind is criminal and delinquent behavior, in which the deviant activity is not of the professional kind.

If our reasoning is valid, we can expect to find that nonprofessional criminals and delinquents are less often committed than most other kinds of deviants, and that when they are committed it has taken longer for this mental state to develop. Unfortunately, so far as this author knows, no such comparative data are available. Nevertheless, recent works by Glaser and Matza indirectly support the proposition that continuance commitment to a criminal or delinquent identity happens in only a small proportion of the cases.[44]

Our observations suggest the hypothesis that the variation in the inevitability of occurrence of kinds of penalties is a factor in the development of commitment. Although the foregoing discussion has dealt only with identity commitment, there is no reason why the same concluding observations cannot be applied to expectation commitment as well.

The Duration of Commitment

For many deviants commitment is not necessarily a lasting aspect of their lives once they have become aware of it. In fact, this is one of the reasons for stating the case of commitment in subjective terms. The deviant feels this way, but this does not always correspond to the actual state of affairs.

We just cited Matza's contention that delinquents generally end their deviant career at maturation, with very few continuing on into adult crime. Glaser believes, on the basis of his data, that much adult crime ends in a similar way—these deviants simply being more advanced versions of adolescent delinquents. "The crimes appear to be either momentary play at being independent, not regarded as a permanent way of life (such as riding in a stolen car), or attempted shortcuts to the destination of independent adulthood." [45] Even deviants attached to their way of life often undergo disillusionment and shifts of interest. There is always the possibility of therapy for alcoholics, gamblers, the mentally ill, and homosexuals. And, of course, some deviance requires youthful vigor, a quality lost with increasing years.

Undoubtedly the same can be said for many other committed identities. The workman committed to his job by a pension plan and seniority arrangements is often relieved of this condition, if in no other way than by retirement. Divorce and remarriage are always possibilities, as is the renunciation of naturalized citizenship. It would seem too that expectation commitment, involving recurrent situations, does not necessarily endure forever. The person may be able to abandon the social circles which enforce the penalties for nonobservance of the expected behavior. The psychological effects of having made a decision can also be reduced by such means as rationalization, compartmentalization, and the like.

It can be hypothesized here that the self-enhancing commitment lasts longer than the self-degrading variety. Underlying this proposition is the assumption that self-degrading commitment, while preferable to certain alternatives in the conventional world, is still undesirable in itself. The mortifying self-conception then acts as a continuation penalty which furnishes a significant part of the pressure to deal with this unpleasant state of affairs. Commitment to an identity or expectation that creates a negative self-image is viewed here as a lesser-evil choice when initially compared with certain alternatives, and as a greater-evil choice when subsequently compared with certain other alternatives. Obviously, the strength of the motivation is an important consideration in determining whether or not the transition is made.

After Self-degrading Commitment

Generally speaking, self-enhancing commitment presents no problem for deviants, in spite of the fact that they are more or less forced to retain their social role. There is little motivation to leave it for reasons of self-conception. Self-degrading commitment, however, presents quite a different situation, with a number of alternatives open to one committed to an identity or expectation in this manner.

First of all, a person motivated by self-degrading commitment has the objective alternative of redefining the values and the continuation penalties associated with the committed identity or committed expectation in such a way that he becomes attached to them. Basically this alters his perception of the balance of penalties. Such a psychological leap from self-degrading to self-enhancing commitment is exemplified by those Negroes who left prison and joined the Black Muslims [46] and by those homosexuals who are staunch members of such homophile organizations as The Mattachine Society and One, Inc.

The individual can also redefine the renunciation penalties associated with the committed identity or expectation in such a way that the severity of their effect is reduced. This alteration of the perception of the total balance of penalties ultimately permits the person in question to abandon his committed position. We are suggesting here that under the pressures of recognized commitment a new definition of the renunciation penalties may develop, one which leads to a greater willingness to endure them. They are reduced in their effect when compared with the continuation penalties.

Redefinition of the penalties in either direction, leading to real acceptance of the committed identity or ultimate rejection, appears to involve reference groups and special persons within them. This probably includes both newly encountered reference groups and resurgent old ones whose influences were temporarily lost. Whichever the case, it is safe to say that the persons with whom the committed individual begins to interact will provide him with certain significant rewards. They may teach him how to adjust to the fact of commitment, offering him rationalizations for his behavior, showing him how to interact with those who are not so identified and how to carry out successfully the activities associated with his status. Or, in the opposite situation, members of the reference group may provide sympathy while the committed person tries to abandon his unwanted identity. They, too, may offer practical instruction on how to succeed in this effort. These groups provide the actor with a meaningful role, one in which he can receive positive evaluation and encouragement for a well-done performance. Concomitantly, he is also likely to be indoctrinated with new values and a new general perspective on life. This new world view helps him further redefine the penalties associated with the identity to which he is committed. This is often just where organizations like Alcoholics Anonymous, Schizophrenics Anonymous, and Synanon Society enter the picture. Yablonsky describes some of these forces as they operate in Synanon Society:

> *Involvement*
> Initially, Synanon society is able to involve and control the offender. This is accomplished through providing an interesting social setting comprised of associates who understand him and will not be outmaneuvered by his manipulative behavior.
>
> *An Achievable Status System*
> Within the context of this system he can (perhaps, for the first time) see a realistic possibility for legitimate achievement and prestige. Synanon provides a rational and attainable opportunity structure for the success-oriented individual. . . .
>
> *New Social Role*
> Synanon creates a new social role which can be temporarily or indefinitely occupied in the process of social growth and development. . . . This new role is a legitimate one supported by the ex-offender's own community as well as the inclusive society. . . .
>
> *Social Growth*
> In the process of acquiring legitimate social status in Synanon, the offender necessarily, as a side effect, develops the ability to relate, communicate, and work with others. . . .[47]

Without really switching to a form of self-enhancing commitment, it is occasionally possible to adjust psychologically to self-degrading commitment. This depends, of course, upon how strong a motivating force the current state of self-degrading commitment actually is for the deviant. Some types of mildly rejected deviants seem to manage this form of adaptation. Lemert, who refers to such persons as "adjusted pathological deviants," cites beggars and the blind as examples.[48] The possibility of subsequent development of character disorders is another consideration under these circumstances. Cormier suggests such a possibility for criminals at what amounts to the commitment stage of their moral career.[49] Successful adjustment apparently depends, in part, on the availability of a role for them to play in the community.

In the same paper Lemert also considers what he calls "self-defeating and self-perpetuating deviance." Among other forms he cites alcoholism, drug addiction, and systematic check forgery as examples of this sort of vicious circle of cause and effect, characterized by an almost complete absence of any durable pleasure for those involved. Finally, if the escape motivation resulting from the state of self-degrading commitment is exceptionally high and none of the alternatives mentioned so far appeal to the committed individual, suicide becomes a prominent alternative. This outlet from commitment has recently been observed among homosexuals.[50]

Undoubtedly there are many other alternatives to self-degrading commitment besides the ones mentioned here. Much, it seems, depends upon the nature of the identity or expectation to which a person is committed. Our earlier discussion of penalty-producing arrangements demonstrates that there are many different ways in which commitment can manifest itself. Extensive research is required in order to isolate the kinds and circumstances of commitment and the various reactions to it.

The assumption undergirding this discussion of reactions to self-degrading commitment is that the undesirability of such a mental state provides an impetus for the individual to reduce the tension created by it. The above-mentioned routes traveled by these committed persons represent the end products of such motivation.[51] Clearly, our earlier statement that only penalties need concern us does not apply to the discussion in this section. We are now dealing with motivation and why people *want* to leave a particular identity, not with why they cannot leave it. Consequently, the rewards of the various alternatives become important considerations. Unfortunately, an extended discussion of the factors which lead people to wish to change identities or abandon an expectation is beyond the scope of our objective, which is to present the rudiments of a theory of forced behavior. The intention in this section is simply to indicate some of the possibilities of overcoming self-degrading commitment. There are barriers to the development of commitment and limits to its duration that must be taken into consideration in a theory of this phenomenon. It is this general fact which is relevant to our interests.

SUMMARY AND CONCLUSIONS

The concept of the subjective career, as contrasted with the idea of the career pattern, has been shown to have considerable potential for organizing the disparate ideas that have grown up around the movement from primary to secondary deviance. Specifically, the turning points which we have called career contingencies can be of predictive value, given the proper amount of research into their nature. The viability of the notion of deviant career is enhanced by recognizing that it is not necessarily a permanent state and that in some cases "second careers" later develop in nondeviant pursuits.

The idea of continuance commitment is especially pertinent to the transition from primary to secondary deviation. Committed behavior is behavior that persists over time and leads the actor to reject otherwise feasible alternatives. Commitment, as a psychological state, has a future reference in that prospective action will be of a certain kind. Commitment is something one gradually becomes aware of, mostly because of the presence of penalties for opting for any kind of behavior or identity other than the "legitimate" one.

Several preconditions must be met before commitment can be said to exist. First of all, arrangements which produce penalties must exist. The following are examples of identity-committing arrangements: certain kinds of legal contracts, bureaucratic arrangements, adjustments to new positions, ceremonies and public judgments, certain situated presentations of self, and investments and renunciation of investments. Public announcement of behavioral intentions, decisions, certain kinds of legal contracts, and cultural expectations are called expectation-committing arrangements.

There are other preconditions. Commitment is grounded in imminent penalties which may be of a biological, psychological, or social nature. Still, despite these costs, the individual objectively has a choice between adopting the identity or expectation which brings them on and the identity or expectation which leads him to avoid them. The subjective balance of penalties determines how the choice will be made; in the case of commitment the choice is unreal because of the wide preferability gap between the alternatives. On the basis of these observations, commitment has been defined as the psychological state of awareness of the relative impossibility of choosing a specified different identity or rejecting a single expectation because of the perceived imminence of the biological, psychological, and/or social penalties. Commitment, however, does not restrain a person from interaction with others in the noncommitted spheres of life or even from brief flirtations with the actual penalties.

Attachment, an idea closely related to that of commitment, differs from it primarily by the fact that one is not forced to enact an expectation or adopt a particular social identity. Yet when attachment to a deviant identity endures until one becomes publicly recognized for such activities, it always involves an element of commitment. Self-enhancing commitment, as we have come to call attachment with an element of commitment involved, is produced in at least two ways: through social penalties from other deviants and members of the conventional community and through psychological penalties involved in giving up a cherished ideological position.

In attempting to locate self-enhancing commitment as a significant stage within the deviant career, it is important to recognize that its placement is ultimately based on the acquisition of specific values and beliefs assimilated in interaction with admired others. The pursuit of these values and beliefs eventually leads to their consolidation in a desired new identity and associated role expectations; this consolidation is facilitated by interchanges with others who hold the same orientations. Somewhere within this process the individual becomes aware of the social and psychological penalties involved in attempting to abandon this line of activity, should he ever desire to do so. Thus a possible career contingency springs up around the recognition of commitment to oneself, significant deviant others, and the values and beliefs of the group. Public recognition of the attached deviant's identity also brings commitment, solely by means of social penalties that may occur either before or after the aforementioned commitment.

In the case of self-degrading commitment the committed deviant lacks any genuine attachment to his identity, making it the most pathetic type of commitment. Here, although there are psychological penalties involved, they are not of the same kind as those found in self-enhancing commitment; instead they involve the threat of imminent mental stress when one gives up certain defensive mechanisms. Biological penalties also exist, along with the usual social costs. It seems that self-degrading commitment can be located at about the same stages in the deviant career as the self-enhancing variety. Both self-degrading and self-enhancing commitment can be considered a kind of penalty and reward, respectively, to be included in the subjective balancing of penalties.

Limits to commitment, which depend in part on the inevitability of occurrence of the penalties associated with certain forms of deviance, also exist. At least one major kind of deviance has a low inevitability of penalties: nonprofessional crime and juvenile delinquency. It has been hypothesized that these deviants are less likely to become committed than other kinds.

Self-degrading commitment can and is likely to be short-lived because of its motivating characteristics. Several routes are open to the deviant who finds himself at this stage in his career, including even the most improbable one, reintegration into the conventional community with the possible establishment of a second career.

A simplified schematic summary of the deviant career is presented in the flow chart.

A FLOW CHART OF COMMITMENT

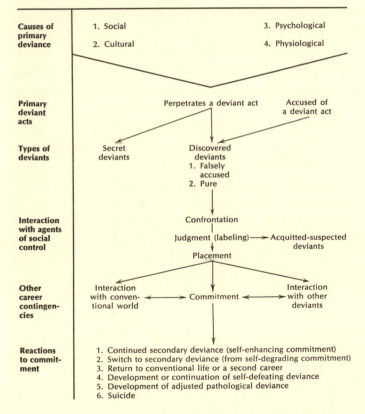

Causes of primary deviance	1. Social 3. Psychological
	2. Cultural 4. Physiological
Primary deviant acts	Perpetrates a deviant act Accused of a deviant act
Types of deviants	Secret deviants Discovered deviants
	1. Falsely accused
	2. Pure
Interaction with agents of social control	Confrontation
	Judgment (labeling) ──► Acquitted-suspected deviants
	Placement
Other career contingencies	Interaction with conventional world ◄──► Commitment ◄──► Interaction with other deviants
Reactions to commitment	1. Continued secondary deviance (self-enhancing commitment)
	2. Switch to secondary deviance (from self-degrading commitment)
	3. Return to conventional life or a second career
	4. Development or continuation of self-defeating deviance
	5. Development of adjusted pathological deviance
	6. Suicide

NOTES

1. Edwin M. Lemert, *Human Deviance, Social Problems, and Social Control,* p. 51.

2. Sigmund Nosow and William H. Form, eds., *Man, Work, and Society,* p. 284.

3. Howard S. Becker, "The Career of the Chicago Public School Teacher," *American Journal of Sociology* 57 (March 1952): 470. This definition was paraphrased by Becker from an earlier work by Oswald Hall. As a definition of the individual-objective view of career, it is preferred to a similar definition given by Becker early in Chapter 1.

4. Erving Goffman, *Asylums,* p. 127.

5. Of course, there are more than even the obvious differences between an occupational career and a deviant career. For instance, there is probably not as much planning even in those deviant careers where the individual is positively attached to his behavior as in certain kinds of professional careers where "career strategies" are likely to exist. See Walter L. Slocum, *Occupational Careers,* pp. 259–262. But this does not mean that we cannot take the term and develop it separately for incorporation into deviance theory. We must be careful, however, that this conceptualization is based upon theoretical and empirical work in the study of deviance and not solely upon the analogical transfer of ideas from occupational sociology. For a more detailed discussion of the subjective nature of career, see the author's article entitled "Career: The Subjective Approach," *The Sociological Quarterly* 11 (Winter 1970): 32–49.

6. Perhaps a better term than recruitment is proselytization, as it is found among political and religious deviants, nudists, and jazz musicians. See John Lofland and Rodney Stark, "Becoming a World Saver," *American Sociological Review* 30 (December 1965): 862–875; Fred Ilfeld, Jr., and Roger Lauer, *Social Nudism in America,* pp. 156–163; Robert A. Stebbins, "The Conflict Between Musical and Commercial Values in the Minneapolis

Jazz Community," *Proceedings of the Minnesota Academy of Science* 30 (1962): 77–78.

7. With the exception of DeLamater, this author knows of no student of deviance who has ventured an opinion as to when the deviant career begins. In the last chapter we theorized that it started with the initial deviant act; DeLamater, on the other hand, holds that it begins with secondary deviation. Although research specifically focused on this problem must be the final arbiter, the concept of subjective career adds a measure of assurance to our own contention. See John DeLamater, "On the Nature of Deviance," *Social Forces* 46 (Fall 1968): 450.

8. The concept of the second career was recently introduced into occupational sociology by Marie R. Haug and Marvin B. Sussman, "The Second Career—Variant of a Sociological Concept" (Paper read at the 61st Annual Meeting of the American Sociological Association, Miami Beach, Florida, September 1966); and Slocum, *Occupational Careers,* p. 242.

9. Several portions of this section first appeared in Robert A. Stebbins, "Commitment, Attachment, and Deviance" (Paper read at the 31st Annual Meeting of the Midwest Sociological Society, Des Moines, Iowa, April 1967).

10. See, for example, J. W. Brehm and A. R. Cohen, *Explorations in Cognitive Dissonance;* and C. I. Hovland et al., *The Order of Presentation in Persuasion.* Some of the time, however, psychologists seem to use commitment to refer to past and therefore irreversible actions. This differs from our formulation in that we are dealing with future behavior where there is always a choice. See Harold B. Gerard, "Deviation, Conformity, and Commitment," in *Current Studies in Social Psychology,* ed. Ivan D. Steiner and Martin Fishbein, pp. 263–277.

11. E. Abramson, et al., "Social Power and Commitment," *American Sociological Review* 23 (1958): 15–22. Howard S. Becker and Anselm L. Strauss, "Careers, Personality, and Adult Socialization," *American Journal of Sociology* 62 (1956): 253–263. Howard S. Becker, "Notes on the Concept of Commitment," *American Journal of Sociology* 66 (1960): 32–40. Erving Goff-

man, *Encounters: Two Studies in the Sociology of Interaction,* pp. 88–90. Howard S. Becker, *Outsiders: Studies in the Sociology of Deviance,* chap. 2. Thomas C. Schelling, *A Strategy of Conflict,* p. 24. Rosabeth Moss Kanter, "Commitment and Social Organization," *American Sociological Review* 33 (August 1968): 499–517.

12. Becker, "Notes on the Concept of Commitment," p. 33.

13. We shall discuss the meaning of the ideas of identity and expectation in greater detail in the next section.

14. Abramson, "Social Power and Commitment," p. 16.

15. Goffman, *Encounters,* p. 89.

16. The reader may be justifiably apprehensive about the risks involved in developing a more general theory of forced behavior from the study of deviance, where presumably the kinds of restrictions mentioned so far are most stringent. The defense against this potential shortcoming is built into our propositional framework, and it is presented in the section entitled "Limits of Commitment." Other qualifications in the characteristics of commitment itself, given before this section, also militate against an overdetermined view of the matter. Finally, it has been the author's impression from his own and others' investigations in deviance that the common sociological view sometimes overstresses the fact of commitment to a deviant identity. The simple antidote to this pitfall is to keep in close contact with the data.

17. Becker, "Notes on the Concept of Commitment," pp. 36–37.

18. By social identity we mean simply the category to which a person is recognized as belonging by the community or some segment of it.

19. Everett C. Hughes, *Men and Their Work,* p. 2.

20. Alfred R. Lindesmith and Anselm L. Strauss, *Social Psychology,* 3d ed., p. 198.

21. Erving Goffman, "On Face Work," *Psychiatry* 18 (1955): 213–231.

22. See Leon Festinger, Henry W. Riecken, Jr., and Stanley Schachter, *When Prophecy Fails,* p. 107.

23. See, for example, Kurt Lewin, "Group Decision and Social Change," in *Readings in Social Psychology,* 3d ed., ed. Eleanor E. Maccoby, Theodore M. Newcomb, and Eugene L. Hartley, pp. 197–211. See Hovland et al., *Order of Presentation,* chap. 3.

24. Leon Festinger, *Conflict, Decision, and Dissonance,* p. 156.

25. Becker, "Notes on the Concept of Commitment," p. 36.

26. Edward E. Jones, *Ingratiation,* p. 30.

27. Societal reactions of this type are to some extent the result of stereotypes of deviants. It is from this observation that J. L. Simmons goes on to note that stereotyping leads to "role imprisonment" or what we have been referring to as continuance commitment. J. L. Simmons, "Public Stereotypes of Deviants," *Social Problems* 13 (Fall 1965): 223–232.

28. The reader may be wondering why we have referred only to penalties and not to rewards. Basically, people are forced to remain in an identity or uphold some expectation because of the bad things that will happen to them if they abandon it. Of course, some of the renunciation penalties will be the absence of certain rewards obtainable only in the committed identity or expectation. The same can be said of continuation penalties, part of which are costs created by the absence of rewards possible only in another identity. But it is not necessary for us to discuss the rewards associated with noncommitted identities, since our aim does not include explaining why people are attracted to them. For further clarification of the place of penalties and rewards in both the value and continuance forms of commitment, see R. A. Stebbins, "On Misunderstanding the Concept of Commitment: A Theoretical Clarification," *Social Forces* 48 (June 1970): 526–529.

29. Howard S. Becker, "The Career of the Chicago Public School Teacher," pp. 470–477.

30. According to Campbell, acquired behavioral dispositions, although known by many different names, all have one common characteristic: they provide coordination of behavior with reference to environmental settings. They are those mental states which develop as a result of certain experiences, and which, be-

cause they are special views of the world, have a particular influence on subsequent behavior. When these predispositions are activated, the individual to whom they belong is conscious of them. Campbell presents a list of over seventy acquired behavioral dispositions, including such seemingly diverse notions as habit, attitude, definition of the situation, sentiment, knowledge, meaning, and concept. See Donald T. Campbell, "Social Attitudes and Other Acquired Behavioral Dispositions," in *Psychology: A Study of a Science,* ed. Sigmund Koch, 6: 94–172.

31. Florian Znaniecki discusses retrospective and prospective definitions of the situation in *Cultural Sciences,* p. 251.

32. This does not necessarily mean that there are more penalties on the commitment side or the noncommitment side, but only that, as a collection of penalties, those which occur when attempts are made to abandon one's committed identity or expectation are more undesirable than the set of penalties endured for staying. Hypothetically, one penalty could be more undesirable than two or three other penalties taken together. This all depends upon how the individual concerned sees it.

33. Harold Finestone, "Reformation and Recidivism among Italian and Polish Criminal Offenders," *American Journal of Sociology* 72 (May 1967): 580.

34. Who knows what modern technology will permit eventually in the way of modification of supposedly immutable biological characteristics? It is apparent from Garfinkle's description of the case of Agnes that the intersexed person does have a choice of the identity, male or female, he adopts. See Harold Garfinkle, *Studies in Ethnomethodology,* chap. 5.

35. William Kornhauser, "Social Bases of Political Commitment," in *Human Behavior and Social Processes,* ed. Arnold M. Rose, p. 329.

36. This is at least suggested, if not partly supported, in the study by Festinger and his associates of a religious cult; greater commitment (here attachment) led to greater self-involvement. See Leon Festinger et al., *When Prophecy Fails,* chaps. 7–8. The author is indebted to Grace L. MacNab for suggesting this point and the reference.

37. This way of stating the matter is not predicated upon the dubious assumption that somehow, in the self-enhancing variety, commitment is more authentic than attachment. Rather, the distinction drawn here is designed to emphasize the fact that commitment is more universal in deviance than attachment, and that this should be made visible in the terminology.

38. Daniel Glaser, "Criminality Theories and Behavioral Images," *American Journal of Sociology* 61 (March 1956): 433–444.

39. Edwin H. Sutherland, ed., *The Professional Thief*, pp. 187–189.

40. There are at least three studies recently completed which point out that jazz musicians are heading toward respectability and away from their earlier deviant identity. See Robert A. Stebbins, "Class, Status, and Power Among Jazz and Commercial Musicians," *The Sociological Quarterly* 7 (Spring 1966): 197–213; Peter C. Pineo and John Porter, "Occupational Prestige in Canada," *The Canadian Review of Sociology and Anthropology* 4 (February 1967): 36; Edward Harvey, "Social Change and the Jazz Musician," *Social Forces* 46 (September 1967): 34–42.

41. See Robert W. White, *The Abnormal Personality*, 2d ed., chap. 11; Roy R. Grinker and John P. Spiegel, *Men Under Stress*, chap. 11.

42. In fact, a considerable amount of research must be carried out before this statement is valid. One has no scientific right merely to assume that the psychological and biological penalties of the deviant committed in a self-degrading way come into awareness at the same point in one's career as the different psychological and interpersonal penalties associated with self-enhancing commitment.

43. Goffman, "On Face Work," pp. 213–231.

44. Glaser's study shows that the rate of recidivism (an index of commitment) is more like 35 percent than the notorious (figure of) 67 percent. See Daniel Glaser, *The Effectiveness of a Prison and Parole System*, p. 20. Matza indicates that most delinquents reform with maturation and that relatively few become

adult offenders. See David Matza, *Delinquency and Drift,* p. 22. These facts do not actually prevent us from talking about commitment among delinquents or adult offenders since, as we shall see shortly, no assumptions will be made regarding the inevitability of lifelong commitment.

45. Glaser, *Effectiveness of Prison and Parole,* p. 471.

46. C. Eric Lincoln, *The Black Muslims in America,* pp. 113–114.

47. Lewis Yablonsky, "The Anticriminal Society: Synanon," *Federal Probation* 26 (February 1962): 50–57.

48. Edwin M. Lemert, *Human Deviance, Social Problems, and Social Control,* pp. 55–57.

49. See Bruno M. Cormier et al., "The Natural History of Criminality and Some Tentative Hypotheses," *The Canadian Journal of Corrections* 1 (1959): 44–45. These authors discuss what they call the criminal's "saturation point," or that phase in his deviant career where he realizes that he is not only unsuccessful in crime but that he also cannot gain entrance to the conventional world. Character disorders are seen as a reaction to this stressful set of circumstances.

50. Edwin M. Schur, *Crimes Without Victims,* p. 100.

51. Lemert, *Human Deviance, Social Problems, and Social Control,* pp. 54–55.

3

THE NONPROFESSIONAL CRIMINAL AND COMMITMENT

The principal focus of this study is the renunciation social penalties endured by certain classes of nonprofessional property criminals. For our purposes the category of "nonprofessional criminal" includes most adolescent delinquents, many of the younger adult offenders, and perhaps certain categories of older offenders. The nonprofessional, as compared with his professional counterpart, lacks any extensive skill in carrying out his unconventional activities, although he is successful enough at the height of his career to make some sort of living by crime. At this stage in his life he is also relatively attached in an ideological sense to the criminal way of life, but this attachment does tend to wane eventually, though sometimes not until early middle age.[1] It is this latter phase of the nonprofessional's life which is of concern to us; that period in his life in which he begins to switch his attachment to the more socially acceptable means of reaching his goals; that period in which self-degrading commitment may be experienced.

Although the distinction between the two groups becomes somewhat blurred in actuality, professional property criminals can be said to exhibit considerable attachment to their work, leading to a positive self-identification in these terms. The most successful possess a good measure of occupational expertise which they apply to such enterprises as pickpocketing, certain lucrative and skilled forms of robbery and burglary, confidence games, and sophisticated shoplifting.[2]

In the last chapter it was argued that because social penalties are less inevitable than the other kinds and because many classes of criminals experience them almost to the sole exclusion of the others, it would seem to be a good place to concentrate attention. For, in spite of the slowness with which social penalties bring on the feeling of commitment, this attitude does, nevertheless, characterize a certain proportion of nonprofessional criminals at a given point in their deviant careers.

Before presenting the study undertaken to investigate the experience of renunciation social penalties among a sample of nonprofessional criminals, it is necessary first to give a general and rough description of the course of the deviant career of those who eventually become committed.

THE CAREER OF THE NONPROFESSIONAL CRIMINAL

First of all, how does this kind of deviant embark upon his antisocial career? Among the many factors that are operative, it has been suggested that a lack of continuance commitment to conventional ways is a condition for "drift" into crime. Matza, who has recently used this concept in his explanation of delinquent behavior, points out that in drift "an actor is neither compelled nor committed to deeds nor freely choosing them; neither different in any simple or fundamental sense from the law abiding, nor the same; conforming to certain traditions in American life while partially unreceptive to other more conventional traditions." [3] The would-be nonprofessional criminal, cut loose from some of the more conventional expectations of the community while at the same time desiring such values as independence, success, and adulthood, finds at least momentary sustenance in minor crime, usually of the burglary, larceny, or auto theft variety.[4]

It seems that many criminals of this kind never get beyond one or two prison terms as a result of their deviant activities.[5] They discover, in various ways, that conventional living is more secure and at least as rewarding. Others, however, continue primary deviant activities that eventually culminate, after repeated judgments from the agents of social control, in sufficient notoriety for them to be presumed publicly labeled. Even at this stage, however, the nonprofessional criminal is not regarded as strongly attached to criminal values and to a deviant way of life. In fact, he seems still to be far more attached to certain values of conventional life (as we mentioned, adulthood, success, and independence) than anything else. He differs only in his chosen means to reach them.

From interaction with conventional members of the community, the nonprofessional criminal who continues in primary deviation comes to learn more and more about the social penalties that accrue as a result of his deviant activities.

The slow rate of accumulation of this knowledge is partly a response to the slow growth of notoriety as a criminal; for example, public labeling takes place with each imprisonment, but it may well take several prison terms and releases for the knowledge to become sufficiently general throughout the community or neighborhood to have an effect upon his life chances. Additionally, social penalties, practically the sole category of penalties for this kind of deviant, are less inevitable in their occurrence than other classes of penalties, a fact which makes the process of learning slower.

In a very real sense the nonprofessional criminal seems still to be in drift during this period.[6] This situation continues until notoriety is so well established that he begins to feel the full effect of the societal reaction.

All the while the nonprofessional criminal views this increasingly clear knowledge of the social penalties in terms of his major desires: certain values of the conventional world. Thus, he eventually comes to recognize that his continued life in crime is not bringing him any closer to these goals. At the same time he may accept the dubious assumption that continued crime only increases his chances of being apprehended again for deviant acts [7]—a situation which would lead to the odious existence of prisoner and a subsequent increase in, or at least maintenance of, community stigma.[8] He also begins to realize that these very activities have, at least partially, generated certain costs or social penalties that make it increasingly difficult for him to adopt a strictly conventional way of life. When the deviant's awareness of these two lines of knowledge come together, self-degrading commitment has set in, and the deviant has reached another contingency or turning point in his moral career.

As we have already concluded, self-degrading commitment includes a motivating quality which drives the deviant
to react to it in certain ways. The possibility of a second
career in conventional life still exists, and even at this stage
of their deviant careers some nonprofessional criminals
manage successfully to shake off their old ways. There are
also other more likely and more prevalent options, such as a
switch to secondary deviance supported by a newly acquired
attachment to professional criminal values, the development
of self-defeating deviance or of adjusted pathological deviance, or in rare cases even suicide.

For those who do attempt once again to reestablish
themselves in conventional circles, the gnawing thought and
the reality of continuous social penalties is always present. If
we may conjecture here, it may be said that these costs, in a
large majority of the cases, impress upon the nonprofessional criminal the idea that he is not much more likely to
be successful in the pursuit of the values of adulthood,
independence, and success in the "straight world" than in the
deviant one. So there is a return to crime once again, a cycle
which is probably repeated many times, the deviant identity
never really being renounced. Furthermore, once the social
penalties are more or less fully recognized, this return is no
longer a drifting back, but a direct reaction to painful situations culminating in renewed deviant activities and associations with other deviants or, at best, with socially marginal
persons.

The inability to achieve adult status, independence, and
success has been found to be rooted principally in the economic plight of the nonprofessional criminal. Glaser learned
that the chief barrier to employment is not the criminal

record, but the individual's lack of extensive and skilled work experience.[9] Work at the unskilled and semiskilled levels is often not available, and when it is, it is highly unsatisfactory in terms of the pay or the nature of the work itself. Glaser concludes that

> over 90 per cent of felony arrests reported in the United States as a whole, and an even higher per cent of recidivist felonies, involve the taking of someone else's money or other property. This, in conjunction with the considerable association between recidivism and unemployment, suggests that the criminal activity which sends men back to prison in the United States is undertaken primarily as an alternative to legitimate gainful employment.[10]

It might be useful at this moment to review just what we mean by the idea of continuance commitment, so that the reader can more clearly see how the nonprofessional criminal who has engaged in considerable primary deviation can be said to be in such a state. Commitment, regardless of kind, is defined as the psychological state of awareness of the relative impossibility of choosing a specified different identity or rejecting a single expectation because of the perceived imminence of biological, psychological, and/or social penalties involved in making the switch. It was emphasized that this is a subjective state; the individual's interpretation of reality is not necessarily an objective view. In addition, the condition of commitment does not prevent the deviant from interacting with nondeviants, but only prevents him from successfully changing his identity or expectation of behavior. In the case of the nonprofessional criminal, commitment does not prevent attempts at reestablishment in the conventional world and perhaps even the achievement of a semiconventional way of life (e.g., the life of the artist or the musician). It does preclude a normal nondeviant way of living at that time. We have also seen that commitment is not an enduring condition, but one likely to be short-lived.

From Glaser's survey it is obvious that the proportion of committed nonprofessional criminals is small compared with the total number who pass through the prisons and take their place once again in society. However, a study of some of the factors involved in their commitment is still justified since it is doubtful that this proportion is so small as to be insignificant. Furthermore, knowledge of the social penalties associated with this kind of deviance may be transferable to other forms as well.

STATEMENT OF THE PROBLEM

We have shown how it is possible for some nonprofessional criminals to become committed to their deviant identity in a self-degrading way. At least one noticeable weakness in this formulation is the proposition that the knowledge of social penalties increases to the point where a feeling of commitment sets in. Just what are these social penalties? What about them is so odious that they can develop a feeling of commitment in the nonprofessional criminal? These questions, among others, must be answered before anything like a complete formulation can be established regarding the nonprofessional criminal and the career contingency of self-degrading commitment. Because of their immediate importance, these questions may be taken as the statement of the research problem of the study reported in the following three chapters.

THE STUDY

To answer these questions about nonprofessional criminals in a preliminary way, twenty-two third- and fourth-time male offenders were interviewed in September and October, 1967, along a variety of dimensions which from prior knowledge were hypothesized to be social penalties.[11] The prisoners, all of whom were incarcerated at one of the institutions in the Newfoundland penitentiary system, fitted the criteria of nonprofessional criminal almost perfectly. All of them had been sentenced to short terms in prison of two years or less for minor property offenses, while some had also been charged with extensive and repeated traffic violations or disorderly conduct. In addition, the respondents were all judged by five of the senior penitentiary staff to have the characteristics typical of that part of their deviant careers which is under consideration in this study: low-level criminal skills, a waning ideological attachment to crime as a way of life, and a burgeoning attachment to a nondeviant mode of living.

In order to obtain a comparative basis from which to view the social penalties experienced by the nonprofessionals, an all-male group of nineteen professional criminals was selected for interview in December, 1968, from among the inmate population at Dorchester Penitentiary in New Brunswick. While the lengths of sentences were considerably longer for the professionals than for the nonprofessionals,[12] most of the former were also third- and fourth-time offenders.[13] To ensure that each respondent was a professional, he had to be unanimously identified as such by a panel of seven judges comprised of the prison psychologists and senior deputy wardens. The criteria for judging were the opposite of those used in locating nonprofessional offenders: high-level criminal skill, presence of considerable ideological attachment to crime as a way of life, and positive self-identification as a criminal. The Dorchester sample was made up almost entirely of "heavy" property offenders of one kind or another. Their offenses were chiefly armed robbery with and without violence; break, entry, and theft; and in one case, fraud. Many were also charged with prison escape at some time during their criminal careers.[14]

Commitment was established in two ways. The first of these concerned the kind of commitment (self-enhancing or self-degrading), and can be said to follow logically from the professional or nonprofessional status of the respondent. That is, a positive or esteemed self-identification is inherent in the label of professional, while a negative or mortifying self-identification is inherent in the label of nonprofessional (at the stage of his career which is of interest to us).

However, beyond the kind of commitment experienced, it was still necessary to determine the prisoner's awareness of this state. This was done by asking each respondent a question specially designed to establish the presence or absence of the feeling of commitment. In all cases this was done at the end of the interview when rapport was assumed to be greatest. The nonprofessional criminals were asked what they thought their chances were of returning to prison at some time in the future. Only slightly over 18 percent were sure that they would never return.[15] The distribution of responses to this question is presented in Table 1. For a large majority of those who stated a condition for their returning, the contingencies focused on some aspect of employment, such as getting a job either inside or outside of Newfoundland or in one case getting an education.

TABLE 1

SUBJECTIVE ESTIMATES BY NONPROFESSIONAL CRIMINALS
OF CHANCES OF RETURNING TO PRISON

ESTIMATE OF CHANCES	Number	Percent
Good chance of returning	2	9.1
Moderate chance of returning	3	13.6
Small chance of returning	5	22.7
Never returning	4	18.2
Conditional	8	36.4
Totals	22	100.0

As we shall see later, the chances of getting some kind of
work in the province appear to be good, but other factors,
of which the nonprofessionals are aware, intervene to make
it unlikely that ex-offenders will obtain and hold jobs. Thus,
those who gave a conditional answer to the question can be
considered committed.

The professional criminals were asked about the likeli-
hood that they would abandon crime as a way of life and go
"straight." The results are presented in Table 2. Only slightly
over 26 percent indicated that there was a good chance of
leaving their criminal way of life. The conditional answers
can be interpreted in the same manner as those of the nonprofessionals: a number of factors intervene which make it
unlikely that the respondents will find acceptable legitimate
employment or avoid associating with deviant acquaintances.

It is possible, of course, that this question asked of the
professional criminals indicates their attachment to that form
of livelihood instead of their awareness of a state of commit-

TABLE 2

SUBJECTIVE ESTIMATES BY PROFESSIONAL CRIMINALS
OF CHANCES OF ABANDONING CRIME

ESTIMATE OF CHANCES	Number	Percent
Good chance of abandoning crime	5	26.3
Moderate chance of abandoning crime	1	5.3
Small chance of abandoning crime	0	0.0
Never abandon crime	4	21.1

Conditional
    Finding acceptable job
    Not seeing criminal friends
	7
	2
		36.8
		10.5

Totals	19	100.0

ment. The impact of the social and psychological penalties leading to commitment is probably a good deal less in the self-enhancing form since those so committed are not considering abandoning the relevant identity and, consequently, have not directly experienced them. Thus, awareness of commitment may be held only dimly.

The interviews, which lasted anywhere from one to two hours, were necessarily quite unstructured owing to the unfamiliarity of the territory. They were conducted in a separate room normally used for interviewing and medical examinations off the main block of cells. This arrangement ensured the required anonymity of responses and concentrated attention more exclusively on the questions being asked and the other exchanges between respondent and interviewer. The author himself carried out the interviewing.

The question of rapport and validity of responses constantly recurs in research of this kind, and it is appropriate to make some comments about the procedures adopted here. It appears that the reliability and validity of response depends upon, among other things, the nature of the questions asked, the kind of data needed, the nature of the respondent, the degree of anonymity, and the degree of rapport. The questions asked in the present study were not of the variety which could send the prisoner to jail for another sentence if answered honestly. The data which was being sought was also information with which the prisoners had firsthand experience and about which they had often well-developed opinions. The interviews provided an opportunity to express their side of the story. Thus, there was little reason to expect the more usual "role calculation" to characterize the respondent's answers, a trait so often found among prisoners in the large institutions.[16] To this it should be added that there is some evidence that at least among rural Newfoundlanders there is an emphasis on the values of harmony, consensus, and non-exploitation.[17] Such values are not congruent with those fostering role calculation.

There are a number of reasons to believe that a high degree of rapport existed throughout most of the interviews. For the Newfoundland sample the legitimacy of the entire transaction between interviewer and respondent was probably greatly enhanced by the unusual presence of the former. From his speech, choice of words, accent, demeanor, and other personal aspects, the respondents had little choice but to conclude that the interviewer was an outsider since these characteristics are missing from their contacts in Newfoundland, including even the agents of social control. The fact that he claimed to be employed at Memorial University in

St. John's was to them a reasonable identification. He also avoided any tendencies to moralize, but clothed the entire encounter in scientific garb.

Finally there is considerable evidence from several studies of various kinds of criminal behavior which indicates that when the above conditions are met, reliable and valid data can be obtained.[18] Although direct participation is essential for some kinds of data in this field, other kinds can be gathered by skillful interviewing with as great or greater efficacy.[19]

This study was not guided by formal hypotheses in the sense of testable propositions derived from a larger body of theory and operationalized for empirical verification. We worked from a single proposition: that there are social penalties attached to being a publicly known nonprofessional criminal. A number of renunciation social penalties were formulated from the relevant literature in the field, and they were put to test in the present research. Again, social penalties are those costs which are imposed upon the individual by other people, whether deviant or nondeviant, and which are distinct from biological and psychological penalties. The main task of this research was to provide evidence with which to reformulate these social penalties to fit the theoretical framework being developed here, as well as to determine if they truly function as costs for the individual deviants. Often they were stated in terms intended to apply to all forms of deviance, our task being then to see if they hold for nonprofessional criminals.

The next three chapters are devoted to a look at some of the renunciation social penalties which committed nonprofessional criminals experience. Chapter 5 deals with material penalties or those costs stemming from the interaction with others in the worlds of work, consumption, and related areas. Chapters 6 and 7 present the penalties gained from interpersonal relations in various other spheres of life.

SUMMARY

The nonprofessional criminal as we have defined him here is numerically by far the most prevalent of the various kinds of criminal deviants. The nonprofessionals are predominantly late adolescent and young adult males (and possibly some older offenders) who have drifted into crime out of a lack of roots in the mores of the conventional part of the community, who at the same time are exceptionally motivated to acquire the generally accepted values of adulthood, independence, maturity, and success.

It is a fact that many nonprofessional criminals never go beyond one or two offenses for which they have been incarcerated or for which they have endured some lesser punishment such as probation, a suspended sentence, or a fine. Others continue their deviant acts, more or less in a state of drift; in doing so they acquire greater public recognition and concomitantly more knowledge about the social penalties associated with swimming against the social current. Still, even in further deviant behavior, the nonprofessional criminal retains in mind the conventional values mentioned above.

Eventually this criminal behavior and awareness of social penalties culminates in self-degrading commitment which has its own stimulating effects. While he wishes to "go straight," the nonprofessional criminal usually finds that by this time the social penalties are too much to endure. Thus, he continues in crime and in his associations with deviant others. The best evidence to date suggests that economic penalties prevent a successful reintegration into the wider community. The present study offers some potential qualifications to this statement.

Only a small proportion of all nonprofessional criminals get to this stage of their deviant careers. Still, it is worth exploring the nature of these social penalties that create the feeling of commitment and how they work to do this. Theoretically, these questions must be answered since they represent a weak link in the theory of commitment. Practically, an adequate answer will provide beneficial data for practitioners in the area of parole, social work, and similar applied disciplines. Although it is only exploratory in its scope, it is intended that the data from the study presented in the next three chapters will provide both some tentative answers to these questions and a wealth of hypotheses for testing in future research.

NOTES

1. Such a classification seems to be justified by Glaser's findings where he concludes that some take longer in learning to satisfy certain conventional adult needs than others. This situation is partly influenced by the fact that some receive more guidance than others, though most eventually learn that crime is a dead end. See Daniel Glaser, *The Effectiveness of a Prison and Parole System,* p. 471. For two similar classifications, see Gibbons'

"semiprofessional property criminal" or Clinard's "ordinary criminal career." Don C. Gibbons, *Society, Crime, and Criminal Careers*, pp. 258–263; Marshall B. Clinard, *Sociology of Deviant Behavior*, pp. 244–245.

2. Gibbons, *Criminal Careers*, pp. 252–257. The professionals in this study conform most closely to Gibbons' "professional heavy" type.

3. David Matza, *Delinquency and Drift*, pp. 27–31. Lemert has stated the drift thesis for deviance in general. See Edwin M. Lemert, *Human Deviance, Social Problems, and Social Control*, pp. 51–52.

4. Glaser, *Effectiveness of Prison and Parole*, p. 471. To the extent that they drift into their identity through a series of deviant acts, it is possible that certain groups of older offenders could also be included in our category of nonprofessional criminal. Lemert's observations on the check forger, for example, indicate that he is anything but a professional as far as his own view of himself is concerned. See Lemert, *Human Deviance, Social Problems, and Social Control*, chaps. 7–9. The same appears to be true of the embezzler: see Donald R. Cressey, *Other People's Money*, chap. 4. As long as these types of criminals do not conceive of themselves as professional and are attached to many of the same values as the more law-abiding members of the conventional community, then they can be placed in the category being developed here—the nonprofessional criminal. Like the delinquents and young adult offenders so far discussed, they deviate from conventional behavior only in the means used to gain certain socially accepted values.

5. Glaser, *Effectiveness of Prison and Parole*, found that "at least 90 per cent of American prison releasees seek legitimate careers for a month or more after they leave prison" (p. 475). "Most persons released from prison avoid further imprisonment for many years or for life, although many of these do not avoid further arrest. . . . If one places a felon in a prison, he is more likely than not to come out no longer a felon, and he is especially likely to come out not immediately a felon" (p. 476). This is

further supported by the low recidivism rate discovered in his samples.

6. This was suggested to the author by John Nicholson in conversation.

7. This belief that continued crime results in increased chances of being apprehended rests upon several assumptions. First of all it presumes that the criminal is recognized or at least suspected by the police as having perpetrated certain deviant acts. It then posits that the police are making a special effort to catch him in his next act of crime. It also assumes that the skill in carrying out these activities remains the same or perhaps even deteriorates for the individual criminal. These are not propositions which can be assumed to be true, but must be verified. Otherwise, the notion that continued crime results in increased chances of apprehension is a case of the "gambler's fallacy": de facto independent events are mistakenly perceived as being influenced by certain preceding events. Subjectively, of course, the criminal himself could believe this yet undemonstrated proposition which could have the effect of psychologically disorganizing his future deviant behavior, leading eventually to a self-fulfilling prophecy. It is on the basis of these reservations that the proposition concerning the increased chances of apprehension is to be, at least temporarily, suspected.

8. Two case histories suggest that this may be true even among the more professional criminals. See Edwin Sutherland, ed., *The Professional Thief*, p. 188; Clifford R. Shaw, *Brothers in Crime*, p. 349.

9. Glaser, *Effectiveness of Prison and Parole*, p. 361.

10. Ibid., pp. 488–489.

11. In the strict sense of the word, these twenty-two prisoners were not a sample at all but the total number of third- and fourth-time offenders serving sentences of one month or more in Newfoundland at that time.

12. For the nonprofessionals the median length of incarceration per sentence was 2.57 months, while for the professionals it was 23.5 months.

13. A small proportion of the professional criminals interviewed had been incarcerated only twice or, in a couple of instances, had been incarcerated seven and eight times. The author found it difficult to get respondents who the judges unanimously agreed were professional and who were at the same time third- and fourth-time offenders. Given the purpose for which the professionals were being interviewed, it was felt to be wiser to compromise on the number of sentences than on the criteria of professionalism.

14. According to Gibbons, the professional heavy type of criminal also tends to retire from his deviant way of life sometime during middle age. However, we will shortly present some evidence which suggests that this retirement may not be complete, but amounts to rejecting only high-risk crimes. The fact that professionals, like nonprofessionals, do tend to abandon crime (whether totally or not) does not invalidate the comparison being undertaken in this study. We are simply trying to demonstrate variation in the experience of penalties; that professionals may undergo the same experiences later in their careers does not destroy the effectiveness of our design. In the meantime, the professionals selected for interview do represent something of an extreme in North American criminality in terms of skills and ideological attachment.

15. Humanistically, the condition of self-degrading commitment is externalized by its possessor in a statement something like the following: "I would like to make it in the straight world, but I doubt that I will do it."

16. The term role calculation has been introduced by John Mitchell to signify the "conscious and deliberate simulation of conformity to demands of power defined as real but not as moral to the person under its control. . . . The person conforms or appears to conform only to evade penalties or to maximize his own individual interest" (See John Mitchell, "Cons, Square-Johns, and Rehabilitation," in *Role Theory: Concepts and Research,* ed. Bruce J. Biddle and Edwin J. Thomas, p. 210).

17. John Szwed, "Private Cultures and Public Imagery,"

Newfoundland Social and Economic Studies, no. 2, pp. 104–105; James C. Faris, "Cat Harbour: A Newfoundland Fishing Settlement," Newfoundland Social and Economic Studies, no. 3, p. 131; Melvin M. Firestone, "Brothers and Rivals: Patrilocality in Savage Cove," Newfoundland Social and Economic Studies, no. 5, p. 130. Slightly under half of the men interviewed came from communities of 6,000 people or less. Furthermore, many of those living in the two cities on the island, Corner Brook and St. John's, are only first-generation urban dwellers.

18. See John C. Ball, "Reliability and Validity of Interview Data Obtained from 59 Drug Addicts," *American Journal of Sociology* 72 (May 1967): 650–654; John P. Clark et al., "Polygraph and Interview Validation of Self-Reported Deviant Behavior," *American Sociological Review* 31 (August 1966): 516–523. Also related are Isidor Chein, *The Road to H*, pp. 112–113, 209; Richard Blum et al., *Utopiates*, chap. 2; P. D. Scott et al., "Delinquency and the Amphetamines," *British Journal of Psychiatry* 111 (September 1965): 865–875; Hunter Gillies, "Murder in the West of Scotland," *British Journal of Psychiatry* 111 (November 1965): 1087–1094.

19. Polsky has provided a spicy account of participant observer techniques and a justification for their use among criminals in Ned Polsky, *Hustlers, Beats, and Others,* chap. 3.

4

THE RENUNCIATION
SOCIAL PENALTIES
OF MATERIAL LIFE

Past research has painted a rather bleak picture of the non-professional criminal's economic life. Bonding companies have usually refused to post bond for men known to have a prison record although some exceptions have recently been found.[1] This is especially true for blanket bonding in such occupations as delivery man, trucker, and warehouse worker. Generally speaking, prison training has not been adequate to meet apprenticeship requirements in the unions.[2] This seems to have less to do with one's prison record than with the perceived quality of training, since a person who had a trade before entering prison usually finds it possible to reinstate himself in his union when he is released. Even where the company concerned would like to hire a man with a criminal record, its officials may find that they are barred from getting licenses for their trucks or their business.[3] Sometimes even the nature of the deviance affects one's chances of getting work; one study found sex offenses to be the most objectionable, stealing from fellow workers the next, and, at least for larger firms, criminal violence being the least serious.[4] These facts point to the general conclusion found in many of the studies of ex-offenders: the greater the amount of training and responsibility required of an employee, the greater the chances of a rejected job application because of a criminal record.[5]

The ex-offender's attitude is often cited as a factor contributing to his dismal economic situation. For instance, it has been found that many have a defeatist attitude toward the possibilities of obtaining a job, a sentiment which seems to be learned from prison ideology and from those who have failed to gain satisfactory employment.[6] It should be noted, however, that other results suggest that socialization to criminal values reaches a peak sometime during the middle of the individual's period of incarceration, and that resocialization to conventional values occurs as the inmate comes to anticipate parole and release.[7] How this affects the defeatist attitude has, to this author's knowledge, not yet been determined. Also, it has been found that the ex-offender has poor work habits in that he finds it hard to conform to regular hours and the demands for a consistent effort,[8] a condition usually traced to the dependency promoted by institutional life and childhood upbringing. Finally, there is some indication that newly released inmates lack the aggressiveness and sometimes the verbal skills needed to procure a job on their own resources. Some have noted that sponsoring by a parole officer or by some other agent is beneficial and improves the person's chances of a successful post-release economic existence.[9]

There is always the question of the "record." Melichercik found that where the prison record is discovered by the employer after the ex-prisoner has been on the job, he is likely to lose that job.[10] Glaser's large-scale survey, however, disclosed that those who were discharged from their jobs *rarely* gave as the reason for this the fact that their prison record was discovered.[11] Whether or not the discovery of the prison record actually does lead to discharge, it is well known that most releasees are concerned enough about its possible effects to be ambivalent about telling their employer of their past. Apparently this is especially true for those who lived and worked in more stable working-class and middle-class neighborhoods.[12]

The findings of the present study are congruent with those of Glaser. Only three of the twenty-two nonprofessionals reported ever being fired because their prison record had been discovered, and about the same number said they were denied jobs for this reason. Most of those seeking work chose not to tell their prospective employer anything about their record (64 percent), while another 25 percent felt or knew for sure that he had knowledge about their past.[13] It is significant that several of the respondents feared that if the employer should find out about their prison record, they would always be suspect if any illegitimate activities were discovered in the organization. A few actually reported quitting their job for this reason. Although the professionals spent noticeably less time in legitimate employment or looking for such work, the findings among them on this theme are almost exactly the same.

This brief portrayal of the ex-offender's economic background suggests three perceived renunciation social penalties:

1. Where a nonprofessional criminal has a known prison record, he will have difficulty finding a job within his personal range of acceptable alternatives.[14]

2. Where a nonprofessional criminal with a known prison record does find a job, it will be at the lower end of the occupational prestige spectrum.

3. Where a nonprofessional criminal with a prison record does find a job, he will have trouble holding it because of poor work habits and the undesirable nature of the work.

EMPLOYMENT OF EX-OFFENDERS

The Newfoundland prisoners were interviewed on matters in their post-release lives which related to these and other social penalties. With respect to the three social penalties presented above, there seemed to be no shortage of work for these released prisoners in Newfoundland or even as far west as Toronto.[15] Although it took an average of eighty-six days before the released prisoner obtained his first job, over 77 percent of those interviewed obtained those jobs on the first attempt. In 35 percent of the cases full-time employment was, in fact, found in fourteen days or less. Parenthetically, almost all of these jobs were procured by the ex-offenders themselves, employment agencies being notoriously unsuccessful at placing them.[16]

However, better than 92 percent of these first jobs, found just after release, were in the unskilled and semiskilled categories, the former being by far the most prominent class of work.[17] Furthermore, 46 percent of these jobs were vacated because they were personally unacceptable in some way, the unacceptability being mirrored in some instances by the job holder returning to prison for another offense.[18] Additionally, 30 percent of those who were seeking jobs said they had turned down employment offers because the work was undesirable, low wages or some unpleasant physical condition of the work being the major reasons. A larger proportion, 40 percent, simply did not apply for certain jobs because they preferred not to do that kind of work. Again, pay and physical conditions of the work were given as the main reasons for rejection.

Various physical conditions were odious to the respondents. In some cases these conditions were simply long or undesirable hours; filling station work, for example, often involves both of these. Occasionally, the work rejected was heavy, such as the kind done in the "lumber woods" or in highway construction. Fishing was also undesirable since it usually involves not only some heavy work but also work in cold weather (and cold water), as well as long hours. Most of the forms of employment which were physically unattractive also appeared to have a low wage scale, especially where the workers were not unionized.

It would seem that in spite of the fact that employment of some kind was available, much of it was undesirable and could be construed as penalizing. Most of the work was not gratifying enough to constitute a factor in commitment to a new identity in the conventional world, and probably for many of these men the work was relatively unglamorous compared even with petty crime as a livelihood. Moreover, their occupational identity was one of low prestige, simultaneously promoting a negative self-conception and yielding meager wages. The work itself was often physically tiring and uncomfortable (like roadwork, lumbering, working in filling stations, etc.), disenchanting them further when they compared this alternative with that of further criminal activity. It would seem then that the nonprofessional criminal in this sample was definitely penalized by his employment situation,[19] a penalty which future research could well show to be a factor in maintaining the deviant identity.[20]

Author Harold Horwood, in a series of articles on Newfoundland criminals and juvenile delinquents published in the St. John's *Evening Telegram,* reported the following observations made by one of his respondents on the utility of the provincial prison camp at Salmonier with respect to legitimate employment:

> [*Horwood*]: You served one sentence at the prison farm in the Deer Park?
> [*Respondent*]: Yeah, most of it, but like I say they didn't teach us nothing. If you could learn how to take down an engine, for instance, or put in time on a trade, or anything that might help you get a job. That's the real trouble, you know. If guys could get jobs and get decent pay and be treated decent, there'd be no repeaters—next to none, anyway, except for a few real nuts that ought to be in the booby hatch. . . .[21]

The most obvious difference, along these lines, between the nonprofessional Newfoundland criminals and the professionals at Dorchester was the noticeable absence of conventional employment and favorable attitudes toward it among the latter. Just over half of the professionals never obtained a job after their several releases from prison as compared with 27 percent of the nonprofessionals. But the number of jobs applied for and the undesirability of the various kinds of legitimate employment indicated that the professionals were not interested in supporting themselves in conventional ways. Low pay was the main reason for avoiding such work. Furthermore, those who did get employment often abandoned it shortly afterward because of the low wages, thereupon returning to crime. However, here also there appeared to be no shortage of available jobs, for when work was desired (such as for parole purposes) they were usually able to find it immediately. The availability of better paying jobs seemed to be facilitated by the learning of a trade behind prison walls, as was indicated by several of those interviewed at Dorchester.

Thus, one of the chief distinguishing characteristics between the professionals and nonprofessionals in this study was the notable lack of interest in legitimate work on the part of the former. While this could easily be predicted from what we have already said about professional criminals, it also points out a difference in experienced penalties between the two groups. Nonprofessionals wanted legitimate work that would pay well, would be reasonably comfortable, and would bring self-respect. Because of their lack of training and low level of general education,[22] they were not able to obtain this sort of employment. This inability to obtain acceptable employment was, in turn, seen as a penalty for abandoning even petty crime as a livelihood or partial livelihood. The professionals, on the other hand, did not experience their lack of legitimate work as a penalty because they had never been very interested in that kind of living in the first place. Even with their somewhat higher level of general education and store of skilled trades, their kind of crime as an economic strategy appeared to them to offer more opportunities.

The professional criminal's attitude toward conventional employment is indirectly summed up in his attitude toward crime itself. Robert Allerton puts it this way:

> So I content myself with the dream—the one that all criminals have—that one day I'll get the really big tickle. They've all got this dream: they're all going to get a big tickle and then they'll turn the game in for ever, set themselves up in a little business somewhere, retire. That's all I can do now, take my time and wait for the chance to come. I've no intention of going straight, I'm just being more careful, that's all. . . .
>
> And if I had it, if it came off . . . I still wouldn't open a business, I still wouldn't settle down and retire. I should squander it all like I've always done. I've had it before, I've had the chances and I've always done that . . . and I know I shall do it again.[23]

PREPRISON DEBTS AS PENALTIES

Another aspect of the material life of the nonprofessional criminal is his indebtedness. A. M. Kirkpatrick has noted that "on release their immunity from pressure to pay these debts ceases and before they have even solved the problem of survival they are under pressure to pay up . . . they frequently start from way behind scratch."[24] In this connection it is of importance to note that the gate money paid upon release from prison is negligible in most cases, especially when one considers the immediate pressures of daily living upon a person who has been incarcerated for a number of years. These pressures include the obvious problems of obtaining food, clothing, and shelter. They also include the fact that most prisoners seem to use tobacco in some form and, presumably, wish to continue to do so once they have regained entrance to the outside world. Association with women in our society is usually a more or less expensive activity for the male involved, and the desire for female companionship is abnormally high just after release. If the ex-offender has little or no money he may be denied this pleasure, while if he attempts to arrange an inexpensive activity he may have to explain why he is in such a predicament. Given the usual shortage of money with which the prisoner enters the community and the nature of his immediate desires, it is no wonder that a sizable debt is interpreted as penalizing.

It would seem, however, that indebtedness from bills incurred before incarceration is characteristic of only a minority of released offenders. Glaser found that only three-eighths of his sample reported having such debts, the amounts ranging from $18 to $290,000 with a median indebtedness of $470.[25] The findings from the present study parallel those of Glaser: roughly 22 percent of the nonprofessionals claimed preprison indebtedness, the range running from $54 to $3,000; while slightly over 42 percent of the professionals were in debt after one of their releases.

The presence of debts incurred before incarceration would function as a renunciation social penalty by demonstrating to the deviant that he would not be faced with them if he could make more money. The penalty would create a feeling of commitment where it was believed that this would not occur if he remained in his deviant identity. We may state this penalty as follows:

4. The presence of preprison debts creates an economic burden, which is perceived as a renunciation social penalty.

As a general social penalty for nonprofessional criminals, however, preprison indebtedness, from the evidence gathered so far, does not seem to be much of a motivating force for any but a minority. One explanation, which might in itself be considered a social penalty, is that it is too difficult for most persons irregularly employed at unskilled occupations to obtain the credit with which to build up any significant debts. Further research into these matters is certainly needed.

PERSONAL AND FAMILY PROPERTY

It has also been found that missing personal and family property is a common fate among released prisoners. Pauline Morris' study of ex-offenders in the London area provides some evidence for this proposition, and comments by Kirkpatrick further support it.[26] Our own results, however, do not lend much weight to the idea: only 13 percent of those interviewed reported any personal or family property missing, and in only two of the three cases were they at all upset by the fact. One respondent claimed to be missing a pair of "long rubbers" or hip boots. Another returned home to find that his wardrobe had been largely taken over by his brother. The third ex-offender found that his treasured shotgun had been sold to help pay for a family member's trip to Toronto.

Just what sort of social penalty missing property can be considered to be is an interesting question, even if it is shown to apply to more than a small minority of deviants. It is not a cost acquired from the nondeviant world for the deviant's attempts to abandon his identity, but rather the reverse. Because he is maintaining a deviant identity and occasionally going to prison for his acts, the deviant finds personal and family property missing. If he were not a deviant he would be at home looking after his own effects. Thus, missing personal and family property is a potential continuation social penalty rather than a renunciation penalty. As such it is outside the scope of the present study.

THE CONSEQUENCES
OF A LACK OF MONEY

Low paying jobs have been labeled a renunciation social penalty because the small amount of money received is in itself a situation of low prestige. If we take the matter still further, inquiring into the consequences of a relative lack of money, we come to recognize still other renunciation penalties. Lemert has observed that without adequate money the deviant cannot formally enter many groups.[27] We may speculate further that his recreational life is greatly hindered in all its aspects. As we saw earlier the ex-offender is likely to be denied some of the meaningful forms of interaction with women when he lacks money. Furthermore, he may be restricted from joining many formal groups, such as labor unions and other voluntary associations. He is probably barred from a variety of forms of leisure from barroom drinking sprees to admission to baseball games. He may find that his transportation situation is affected in that to buy and operate an automobile requires a regular income and any other mode of conveyance is woefully inefficient. Kirkpatrick

has emphasized the effect of a lack of money on the reforming criminal who must support a family.[28] The ex-prisoner
soon learns more vividly than most that modern society requires money for nearly every activity that human beings
care to engage in.

Lack of money becomes a renunciation social penalty
if the nonprofessional criminal comes to feel that there is
better remuneration in crime or that the lack of money can
at least be partly alleviated by supplementary crime. Either
way, further deviance is a mode of retreating from the personal
costs associated with low monetary resources.

5. The condition of a low amount or virtual lack of
   money often met by the deviant trying to abandon a
   nonprofessional criminal identity is perceived as a renunciation social penalty.

For the most part the results of the present study support
this hypothesis. Only 31 percent of the nonprofessionals answered that they had an adequate amount of money during
their periods of release from prison. The remainder were
either always without enough money or without it only when
they were unemployed. But in this connection most of the
sample was without work for a considerable portion of the
time between prison sentences.[29] Exactly 50 percent of those
Newfoundlanders interviewed reported that they had been
on relief at least once, the median length of time being
slightly better than twelve weeks. This figure is made more
significant by the fact that six of the respondents were eighteen
years of age or younger and lived at home for various periods
of time after their release from prison and, therefore, had
no claim to relief payments.

Only four of the twenty-two nonprofessional respondents were married during any one of their periods of release from prison. However, three of these four claimed to have considerable difficulty supporting their families, even though in two of the cases this consisted of only the respondent and his wife.

Finally, a substantial minority of the nonprofessionals (40 percent) said that, on release, they felt a desire to make up for the time lost while in prison, time which could have been used to get those things they felt others in their walk of life had.[30] Only one-third of these respondents said they were actually able to do this, with lack of desirable employment being the key factor which prevented the remaining two-thirds from attaining this goal. The proportion of those who felt this desire might well have been higher had not so many of the prison sentences been only a month or two in duration—too short to have experienced the feeling of having lost any time. In this connection, a large number of the professionals, twelve out of nineteen (over 63 percent), reported a desire to make up for the lost time. This was accomplished largely by concentrated criminal activity and subsequent high living.[31]

Another continuation social penalty is presented by Morris in her study of the families of prisoners and ex-prisoners. She found that the erstwhile inmate returned to discover that his family's material and health conditions had worsened considerably.[32] This could be perceived as a continuation social penalty to be weighed against the aggregate of renunciation penalties. However, as Morris suggests, it might also cause resentment, thus stimulating further deviant behavior. Of the four respondents who were married at one time or another during their criminal careers, only two were married at the beginning of one of their periods of release from prison. Neither of these two men noticed any deterioration of his family's material or health conditions. One, in fact, admitted that his family lived better in his absence because they were able to draw government welfare payments.

SUMMARY AND CONCLUSIONS

With respect to the nonprofessional criminal's material life, at least five perceived renunciation social penalties may be considered hypothetically as promoting a feeling of commitment to the deviant identity. They are listed below:

1. Where a nonprofessional criminal has a known prison record, he will have difficulty finding a job within his personal range of acceptable alternatives.
2. Where a nonprofessional criminal with a known prison record does find a job, it will be at the lower end of the occupational prestige spectrum.
3. Where a nonprofessional criminal with a prison record does find a job, he will have trouble retaining it because of poor work habits and the undesirable nature of the work.
4. The presence of preprison debts creates an economic burden which is perceived as a renunciation social penalty.
5. The condition of a low amount of or a virtual lack of money often met by the deviant trying to abandon a

nonprofessional criminal identity is perceived as a renunciation social penalty.

In accordance with our conceptualization of the idea of the renunciation social penalty, the evidence suggests that those penalties presented above impress upon the deviant the idea that they would not have been incurred if behavior related to his deviant identity had been continued. Consequently, these penalties impress upon him the fact of his commitment.

Considerable evidence from the present study and those of the past lend support to the first three penalties. The fourth penalty, although salient for some of the Newfoundland sample, does not seem to be general to the class of nonprofessional criminals. The results of Glaser's research lend further confirmation to this observation. One explanation for the relative lack of preprison debts is the difficulty of obtaining credit when irregularly employed in unskilled labor.

The fifth penalty focuses on the negative consequences associated with the low monetary resources promoted by nondeviant pursuits as contrasted with the more remunerative possibilities in crime. The present study provided moderate support for this contention.

In the process of examining the field of renunciation social penalties in the material life of the nonprofessional criminal, we also considered one or possibly two previously reported continuation penalties. One of these, missing personal and family property discovered upon release from prison, received only a very small amount of support from the Newfoundland study. It is considered a continuation penalty because it arises from the individual's absence through imprisonment caused in turn by his deviant behavior. Also, the discovery by the returning ex-offender that his family's material and health condition has worsened can be interpreted in this same manner. This situation was found to be universally true among Morris' respondents in England. There was no supporting evidence for this penalty from the present study.

Despite the possibility of interpreting these last two conditions as continuation social penalties, an opposite conclusion can be reached with equivalent ease; namely, both of these personal and/or family conditions can also cause extensive resentment in the ex-offender. According to this interpretation, he would see society as the blameworthy culprit and respond by further deviance. Thus, even if we decide to label these as continuation penalties, they still cannot be considered antideviant penalties which would push the nonprofessional criminal toward a conventional way of life. The sentiment of resentment would seem to have the opposite effect. Obviously more research is needed before the issue can be conclusively settled.

In the present study, none of these five arrangements were perceived as renunciation penalties by the professional criminals. They were not interested in legitimate employment, so that costs associated with the pursuit of this sort of activity were not experienced. Some of them did have preprison debts, but either they paid them off by means of illegitimate funds or they simply ignored them. Being already outside the law, their indebtedness to a legitimate source made little difference to them.

A balance of renunciation penalties favoring the maintenance of one's criminal identity can be interpreted in this study as retaining the nonprofessional in criminality as some form of livelihood, as an alternative to legitimate means of reaching such goals as adulthood, success, and independence. The view that certain arrangements in both the conventional and deviant worlds are penalizing is taken here as a subjective reaction by the nonprofessional criminal to his "opportunity structures." He has two such structures, one legitimate and the other illegitimate; the former is seen as considerably less desirable than the latter when viewed in terms of the social costs of material life, and the latter is only a lesser-evil choice.[33]

NOTES

1. John Melichercik, "Employment Problems of Former Offenders," p. 8. For the exceptions to this state of affairs, see Arthur F. Lykke, "Attitude of Bonding Companies Toward Probationers and Parolees," *Federal Probation* 21 (December 1957): 36–38; A. M. Kirkpatrick, "After-Care and the Prisoner's Aid Societies," in *Crime and Its Treatment in Canada,* ed. William T. McGrath, p. 395.

2. Kirkpatrick, "After-Care and the Prisoner's Aid Societies," in *Crime and Its Treatment,* ed. McGrath, p. 395.

3. Ibid.

4. J. P. Martin, *Offenders as Employees,* p. 128.

5. Melicherick, "Employment Problems," p. 3; Pauline Morris, *Prisoners and Their Families,* p. 290; Martin, *Offenders as Employees,* p. 73.

6. Jerome H. Skolnick, "Toward a Developmental Theory of Parole," *American Sociological Review* 25 (August 1960): 544; W. Jerry Head, "Job Finding for Prisoners," *Federal Probation* 16 (March 1952): 23.

7. Stanton Wheeler, "Socialization in Correctional Institutions," *American Sociological Review* 26 (October 1961): 708.

8. Elmer Hubert Johnson, *Crime, Correction, and Society,* p. 644; Morris, *Prisoners,* p. 290; Bernard F. McSally, "Finding Jobs for Released Offenders," *Federal Probation* 24 (June 1960): 15.

9. Martin, *Offenders as Employees,* p. 124; Head, "Job Finding," p. 23.

10. Melichercik, "Employment Problems," p. 6.

11. Daniel Glaser, *The Effectiveness of a Prison and Parole System,* p. 353. As we shall see, the evidence from the present study is consistent with these findings, which suggests that Melichercik's results may have to be defended on grounds other than national or societal differences.

12. Ibid., p. 352.

13. It is quite probable that even more than 25 percent of the jobs were obtained in the employer's knowledge of the ex-offender's prison record. Even where the person goes to another community to find work, he could easily be checked upon since kinship and social networks are very extensive throughout the island. If the employer were at all suspicious that he had an ex-offender as an applicant (he could become suspicious by an awkward gap in the applicant's work history, for example), he would have little trouble finding someone who knew a person in the ex-prisoner's home community, if he himself did not know someone there. The unfortunate part of learning about a man's record in this fashion is the reliance upon a local and possibly badly biased interpretation of his character and activities. Probably only those living in St. John's since birth or early childhood can escape this plight, the population of the metropolitan area of that city being 90,838 in 1961.

14. Lemert discusses the importance of the personal range of acceptable alternatives in several aspects of the deviant's life. See Edwin M. Lemert, *Social Pathology,* pp. 86–87.

15. It should be interjected here that many of those interviewed had either worked in Toronto or hoped to go there in the future to work. This pattern is not just limited to criminals, but

is found among nondeviants in various parts of the island. See, for example, Paine's study of Twillingate and Lewisporte: Robert Paine, "Manpower Mobility Study, Summer 1967, Newfoundland Section," pp. 17, 23, 28. See also Dewitt and Wadel's investigation of similar patterns on Fogo Island and Change Islands: Robert DeWitt and Cato Wadel, "Resettlement and Redevelopment: A Study of Notre Dame Bay." There is also evidence that many of both criminals and noncriminals later return home. Apparently, for noncriminals, disillusionment is a factor in the decision to return. For Twillingaters, the availability of employment and urban goods in the metropolis is not sufficient to make the latter seem especially desirable. (Paine, "Manpower Mobility," p. 27). These facts should not lead us immediately to the conclusion that nonprofessional criminals in Newfoundland are *not* leaving because of intolerable social pressures in their home communities in response to their deviant activities. We still do not know the relative proportions with which criminals and noncriminals leave the province for Toronto and with which they return. Until we have such data we can only conjecture.

16. Glaser found a similar situation in his investigation. See Glaser, *Effectiveness of Prison and Parole,* p. 349.

17. Although Newfoundland prisoners can get further primary and secondary education and some informal tradeschool training, practical vocational schooling leading to a certificate and improved chances in the world of work is noticeably lacking. See "Report for the Canadian Committee on Corrections," pp. 3–4.

18. It should be added that another 43 percent of these first jobs after release were terminated because of the practice of laying off employees or because the season or the job itself had ended. Although they were not questioned directly about their feelings on these events, it may be presumed that they saw them as undesirable and penalizing.

19. Again, a similar conclusion was reached by Glaser, *Effectiveness of Prison and Parole,* pp. 488–489.

20. Although there was no sign of it among those interviewed in the present study, Kirkpatrick asserts that the criminal

is often exploited by unscrupulous employees and company officials. If this were found to be sufficiently general among ex-offenders, it could be interpreted as a renunciation social penalty. See A. M. Kirkpatrick, "The Human Problems of Prison After-Care," rev. ed., p. 6.

21. Harold Horwood, *The Evening Telegram* (St. John's, Newfoundland), 4 April 1967, p. 23.

22. The nonprofessionals had an average of 6.9 years of education ranging from Grade 3 to Grade 10 as compared with an average of 7.7 years for the professionals whose range extended from no formal schooling at all to five years of college. Eleven of the nineteen men interviewed at Dorchester had learned one or more trades while serving their sentences. However, only four of these were licensed or unionized.

23. Tony Parker and Robert Allerton, *The Courage of His Convictions,* pp. 190–191.

24. Kirkpatrick, "The Human Problems of Prison After-Care," p. 7; Morris, *Prisoners,* p. 294.

25. Glaser, *Effectiveness of Prison and Parole,* p. 341.

26. Morris, *Prisoners,* p. 294; Kirkpatrick, "The Human Problems of Prison After-Care," p. 7.

27. Lemert, *Social Pathology,* p. 84. He also noticed in connection with this observation that conspicuous expenditure of money is a prestige and success indicator which has a white-washing effect upon one's disreputable identity. To the extent that a lack of money denies the deviant this opportunity and is viewed by him as doing just that, we can also speak of its penalizing effects.

28. Kirkpatrick, "The Human Problems of Prison After-Care," p. 7; Morris, *Prisoners,* p. 296.

29. The respondents were simply asked whether or not they felt they had an adequate amount of money to support themselves and their families and to maintain a satisfying recreational life. What counts here is their interpretation of their financial condition and the perception of it as a renunciation penalty, not the objective state of affairs. It is probably true that most people

in the affluent society, regardless of station, feel that they need more money to live "properly." The hypothesized difference is that the nonprofessional criminal interprets this situation as a penalty for renouncing his deviant identity.

30. This variable is suggested by Kirkpatrick, "After-Care and the Prisoner's Aid Societies," p. 397.

31. Outside of this desire to make up for lost time, the professionals did not differ significantly from the nonprofessionals. They reported overwhelmingly that legitimate employment was an inadequate source of money, but this is to be expected from their general rejection of that sort of activity. Only four of them were married at any time during their releases from prison. These men had no trouble supporting their families, however, since they accomplished this illegally.

32. Morris, *Prisoners,* p. 296. She found the worsening of material conditions of the family to be universally present in her sample.

33. The idea of the opportunity structure was first developed and applied to juvenile delinquency by Richard A. Cloward and Lloyd E. Ohlin, *Delinquency and Opportunity,* p. 152. Unfortunately, this notion was conceptualized as an explanation for acts of initial primary deviance and not for secondary or near-secondary deviance, which is our concern in this study. This has led to considerable research upon the earlier stages of the deviant career from this perspective. Obviously the legitimate opportunity structure changes extensively with public labeling, and some of these changes have been noted in this chapter. What is needed is a reformulation of this theory of delinquency to include changes at later stages of the moral career, and an amount of research equivalent to its initial version.

5

RENUNCIATION SOCIAL PENALTIES IN INTERPERSONAL LIFE, I

While there has been considerable research into what we have referred to as renunciation social penalties in the material life of the nonprofessional criminal, quite the opposite situation exists with respect to his other interpersonal relations. The importance of this residual set of social penalties is delineated in the following formulation: social penalties stemming from the deviant's material existence commit him to a deviant livelihood while social penalties stemming from other interpersonal relations commit him to interaction with other deviants and their sympathizers.[1]

It is this second category of renunciation penalties which is the focus of this and the following chapter. The publicly known deviant carries the knowledge of his stigma with him wherever he goes; as one respondent in the present study put it, "you never forget that you are an ex-con." At the same time he is at that stage in his deviant career where he is simultaneously interacting with members of the conventional world and with other deviants and sympathizers. He is at a stage where he is weighing the costs of his various alternatives.

Some significant proportion of the countless interaction situations of everyday life contain actual and potential threats to the psychological well-being of the deviant who is attempting to regain a conventional standing in the community. These threats, which we call renunciation social penalties, must be dealt with, and we contend that after a certain phase of the deviant career the strategy of coping becomes one of remaining in one's deviant identity. This strategy signifies continuance commitment for the individual, but as far as he is concerned at *that* moment it is the lesser of two evils.

RELATIONS WHERE RECORD IS KNOWN

Zeitoun has observed that after prison there is a general anxiety about the unknown. Phrasing the matter for parolees, he says that "having been removed from society for some time and deprived of his liberty, it is natural for a parolee to develop some anxiety upon his return to the community. His fear of the unknown could easily upset his sense of equilibrium and the longer his confinement is the more his anxiety will be." [2] Such feelings are, of course, focused on situations of what Goffman calls "mixed contact," where deviant and non-deviant meet to transact the business of everyday life. Thus, "the very anticipation of such contacts can of course lead normals and the stigmatized to arrange life so as to avoid them. . . . Lacking the salutary feed-back of daily social intercourse with others, the self-isolate can become suspicious, depressed, hostile, anxious, and bewildered." [3]

The present study tested some of the more specific propositions associated with the problems of mixed contacts between nonprofessional criminals and members of the conventional community. The general hypothesis was that anxiety stemming from the anticipation of negative contacts with nondeviant others is a social penalty which the deviant would not have to endure if he associated only with those who understood his plight: namely, other deviants and assorted sympathizers.

Potentially one of the most unsettling experiences a deviant could suffer would be to have others who know of his prison record invade his privacy by questioning him about various aspects of his moral behavior.[4] Eighteen out of the twenty-two nonprofessionals interviewed in the present study reported that they had been questioned by acquaintances whom they did not know very well about aspects of their criminal life. Most commonly the inquiries were of the variety: "What's it like in prison?" "What did you do?" and occasionally morally tinged questions like, "Are you sorry?" and so forth. A small percentage of the respondents found women to be more inquisitive than men on these matters and, therefore, less restricted in their probing.

Of the eighteen who experienced this kind of questioning, over 72 percent admitted that they did not like such behavior on the part of others. The most usual reaction was to talk about their moral career, in spite of the embarrassment involved. But others would try to change the subject, refuse to talk about it, or even leave the situation. Many would give the examiner a long and exaggerated story if he kept up his questioning too long.[5] Much seemed to depend upon the respondent's definition of the situation: if the questions were not seen as belittling they were psychologically easier to answer than if they were interpreted as morally loaded and condemning. The sentiments of the nonprofessional criminals are evident in the following verbatim comments:

> I am ashamed. I prefer not to talk about it.
>
> I don't try to change the subject unless there is someone around who I do not want to know about it.
>
> I don't like to answer. I don't want it to get around.
>
> I usually tell them that I'd rather not talk about it. If that doesn't work, then I'll walk away.

The five interviewees who reported that they did not object to such questioning could, perhaps, be considered as moving toward the status of adjusted pathological deviant, one of the alternative reactions to self-degrading commitment suggested in Chapter 2.

Goffman has theorized that the deviant may become uncomfortable in his knowledge that his presence makes the conventional members of the encounter uneasy.[6] It is possible that the deviant recognizes that these nondeviants feel humiliated by the fact that he is associating with them, that his stigma is contaminating their image in the community. He may also sense that conventional members of the encounter lack poise when interacting with people like him; they do not know what to say or how to act, overwhelmed by the knowledge that they are confronting a live criminal. They may wish to be pleasant, perhaps because of enlightened attitudes of their own, but they are afraid of hurting the deviant's feelings should they respond in the wrong way or ask improper questions. The "straight" people in the setting may also be curious about the criminal way of life, and find they are barely able to keep this interest out of the conversation. The ex-offender may or may not be aware of these problems for the others present. If he is, and if he is also conscious of their anxiety over being unable to cope with them, he too, may become uncomfortable.

Those in the Newfoundland sample were questioned on this issue, but the results were inconclusive. They are presented in Table 3. Since the questions asked in this connection

TABLE 3

THE NONPROFESSIONAL'S VIEW OF HOW
NONDEVIANTS FELT WHEN HE WAS PRESENT

PERCEIVED FEELINGS	Number	Percent
Their status **was threatened**	6	27.3
Their status **was not threatened**	9	40.9
Their status **was enhanced**	1	4.5
They were **cautious**	1	4.5
Don't know	5	22.8
Totals	22	100.0

appeared to be well understood, the variation in answers may possibly be explained by differences in role-taking ability.[7] Before we can provide any definitive answers to this question, research must be undertaken to determine how nondeviants actually feel about such encounters so that we have some basis for comparison when studying the deviant's point of view.

Known deviants often have to endure a certain amount of staring, the amount depending, of course, upon the noticeability of their distinguishing characteristics.[8] In the present study it was found helpful to classify the stares the respondents received into curiosity stares, hate stares, and recognition stares. Staring of any kind usually makes one somewhat uncomfortable, but curiosity and hate stares and certain forms of recognition stares carry with them something more than that. They contain implicit value judgments about the person stared at; they hold attitudes which are communicated in subtle ways by the starer. Curiosity stares can carry either positive or negative feelings, as in the case of adolescents staring at a teen-age musical idol or in the case of conventional members of the community staring at a known ex-offender to see what a "jailbird" looks like. Hate stares would seem to be further along the same continuum of disgust and dislike than the negative curiosity stare. Probably this stare is, more than anything else, a form of social control, a way of communicating one's disapproval of something another person is or did or stands for. All staring, it has been observed, is a violation of the rule of "civil inattention"; it indicates that one person (the starer) needs more information about another than is available from the socially acceptable quick glance.[9]

Only two of the twenty-two nonprofessional respondents felt they had encountered hate stares, while twelve more claimed to have witnessed curiosity stares. All of those who were treated in this manner disliked it, but most often they reacted simply by staying in the situation and enduring it. Others, however, left the setting, and in two cases actually challenged the starer by asking what it was that he was staring at.

More than two-thirds of these respondents experienced recognition stares just after being released from prison. These stares were disliked intensely since they occurred at a time when the respondents preferred to remain isolated or at least anonymous. Many reported feeling conspicuous, a feeling perhaps best summed up in the remark, "Oh! he's out again." It is possible that the actual proportion who experienced staring is higher than the results show if understanding and reacting to the question can be taken as a reliable index. All the respondents immediately appreciated what the interviewer was after, responding in a way that betrayed firsthand experience. That certain kinds of staring are a penalty for at least some nonprofessional criminals is demonstrated in remarks like: "I felt some self-consciousness and embarrassed —I will never get used to it." "I hate it—I go over and ask them what they're staring at." Clifford Shaw's jack roller, Stanley, reported the following when recalling his train ride home from the penitentiary: "The stares of the passengers on the train burned through me as if to read that I was an ex-convict, just—a jailbird, to be feared and avoided. My feelings burned, but I philosophized. 'I don't give a damn; I'll show them someday.' " [10]

Closely related to the anguish of being stared at is the experience of having humiliating remarks made directly to one's face or audibly and intentionally behind one's back. Sixty percent of the twenty-two nonprofessionals interviewed reported that this had happened to them. The common reaction here, since the remark was perceived as intentional, was to get angry, although several tried to retain their equilibrium by attempting to change the subject, by laughing off the remark, or by some other device, such as simply standing and taking the insult without resistance. Again, to report Stanley's feelings:

> The fellows knew that I had done time, was an ex-convict and they let it be known by making remarks about me when my back was turned. I overheard their remarks and they peeved me. Many times I got into brawls on that account. They often said, "watch out for that jailbird, he has taking habits." Often when I would go into the clubhouse some fellow would say, "Hands on your pockets, here comes the crook!" I tried to mix with them and spent my money lavishly. I was ignorant of the way of boys on the outside of jail like these, and they looked upon me as a "dumb-bell" or "chump" that one could do anything with. . . . I had to grin and bear it, but in my heart I hated them and the whole world and began to be disgusted. I wanted to make good, but the tide was beginning to rise against me again.[11]

Another possible renunciation social penalty associated with nonprofessional criminality is the decline of social skills which often occurs with repeated incarcerations of considerable length.

> While he remains in prison the individual seldom has recourse to the more subtle social skills; tact, insight, and accurate judgment of the attitudes and reactions of other people, so necessary to men and women in the ordinary world, are rarely needed. After prolonged and repeated imprisonment, a man's social reactions become blunted; he is clumsier, less perceptive, and much less confident in his dealings with others. . . . At the same time his relation-

ships with his family and friends generally become attenuated and unreal.[12]

This seems to manifest itself in numerous ways. Not only
does the ex-offender who has served repeated and lengthy
sentences find it difficult to converse with the more practiced
conventional members of the community, but it is claimed
that he also finds it difficult to bargain for proper work loads
and pay.[13] Furthermore, he may be uneasy and ill-adjusted
among women and children.[14]

Unfortunately, the nonprofessionals interviewed in the
present study about their social skills in interaction with nondeviants were rarely in prison long enough for the predicted
effects to become manifest. Most of them felt that their con-
versational ability was as good as ever; and only two of the
respondents reported feeling uncomfortable in the presence
of women and children. Only 15 percent said they felt uneasy
about asking for better work loads or raises in pay, a sentiment which might, in fact, pertain to any late adolescent who
still does not have enough personal confidence to be aggres-
sive at the right times. The data gathered, then, do not support
the proposition about social skills presented above, although
we do not seem to have met an essential precondition, namely,
that prison sentences be of considerable length. It is of interest
in this regard that just over half of the professionals, all of
whom had had long sentences, did experience a deterioration
in social skills.

One consequence of the search for data on the social
skills of criminals was the serendipitous finding that all the
respondents, professional and nonprofessional alike, felt a
certain amount of shame and embarrassment immediately
upon release from prison. This was generally true only after

the first and second sentences. In fact, most ex-offenders tried to avoid others during this period, which appeared to last anywhere from one to four or more weeks. The significant part about this is the observation, contrary to that of Goffman presented at the beginning of this chapter, that a vast majority of the respondents eventually adjusted to the outside world and went about their daily affairs more or less as before. At least they did not remain in isolation as many did in the early weeks. Also significant is the fact that shame and embarrassment were not felt nearly as acutely, if at all, immediately after the third release from prison, a development which again suggests that some of the nonprofessional sample were moving in the direction of adjusted pathological deviance as a reaction to commitment.

Another possible penalty resulting from the attenuation of interpersonal skills, mentioned by Trasler, is the difficulty of sustaining old interpersonal relationships and developing new ones after prison.[15] The present study can provide no data for this proposition, although it should be noted that Glaser's survey revealed that 70 percent of those interviewed in his Post-release Panel made new friends after being released for a median of five months. Even this evidence may be inconclusive, however, since the median length of sentence of those in the effective sample was only 24.8 months, probably not long enough to markedly destroy one's interpersonal skills.[16] The professionals in our study showed no difficulty in maintaining those relationships they desired. This was made easier because, as we shall see shortly, they tended to avoid nondeviants.

Goffman has noted that the deviant may experience considerable uneasiness when forced to interact with conventional members of the community with whom he is only very casually acquainted but who *do* know of his criminal record.[17] Perhaps the most common example of this kind of situation is to be found in the relationships between the ex-prisoner and his new work colleagues. Such encounters could also occur in any number of other places, as in one's leisure activities, in exchanges with certain people in the neighborhood, and perhaps even at home with particular visitors or distant relatives. The deviant does not know what the feelings of these casual acquaintances are toward people like himself, since knowledge of this sort is usually found only in more intimate interpersonal relationships. He is aware, nevertheless, that the public in general harbors various attitudes toward those who break the law, ranging from sympathetic tolerance to vicious rejection. From his past experience he is also aware that these attitudes are frequently translated into behavior consonant with them; so that some of those whom he meets casually will say nothing of his past and treat him without prejudice, while others will eschew contact with him at every opportunity and, when unavoidable in the same situation, will make degrading comments about his character and activities, whether or not either of these is related to his criminality.

Of those interviewed in the Newfoundland study more than 86 percent claimed to have been in such a situation, and, of these, over 68 percent reported being apprehensive about the kind of treatment that might befall them. Their sentiments were voiced in statements like: "Thought they might treat me hard," "I would test them to see how they would treat me," "I was afraid they wouldn't trust me." One respondent remarked that "people just don't know how to treat ex-convicts. Once, when I was going in for the second time, a person came up and shook my hand. Squares, for a joke, will say, 'the cops are after you,' while you are walking down the street."

It has also been suggested by Goffman that nondeviant members of the community may, in subtle ways, undermine the deviant's usual scheme of interpretation of everyday events.[18] This seems to be accomplished in one or both of two ways: (1) minor accomplishments of the deviant person are viewed as remarkable, (2) minor failings are seen as an expression of his deviance. To the extent that this kind of treatment annoys the deviant it can be considered a renunciation social penalty, since it would not exist if he associated only with those sympathetic with his predicament.

The results from the present study do not, unfortunately, provide any substantial support for these assertions. Only two of the nonprofessional respondents reported that any of their minor failings were viewed as expressions of their deviance, whereas four said their minor accomplishments were seen as remarkable. As far as the failings were concerned, one respondent was informed by his parents that his supposedly exceptional interest in sleeping was clearly associated with his criminality, while the other who claimed to be a moderate drinker and smoker found this behavior explained in a similar way by relatives. Accomplishments viewed as remarkable for the ex-offenders included an interest in reading novels, having an occupational skill, and, in one case, actually holding a job for six months on a wager from a girl's mother that this was beyond the capabilities of the individual in question.

While it is possible that more would have responded in the affirmative to these questions had the interviewer been able to formulate more adequate examples of what was meant, the findings among the professionals where abundant and meaningful examples were used were no more encouraging. Only with reference to minor accomplishments, where eight (42 percent) of the respondents had such an experience, was there any evidence that this kind of situation might merit further study. However, only three of the eight reported being even mildly upset about such a transaction with nondeviants.

Generally, the professionals, when compared with the nonprofessionals, lacked any extensive experience in the kinds of situations discussed in this section. They seemed either to prefer or to seek of necessity the company of fellow criminals. This does not mean, of course, that they never came into contact with "squares," but only that they came into contact with them less often and under different circumstances than men trying to establish themselves in the conventional world. They appeared to desire the anonymity afforded by the metropolitan milieu, such as that found by John Martin in a rooming house in a former bohemian district in Chicago:

> I'm living in that same rooming house. It's clean and handy and accessible to everything that you'd care to do. . . . Most everybody there has a tendency to mind their own business. Probably fifty or sixty other people live in the rooming house. I don't know who they are. They don't know my background. . . . A lot of times I've weighed the advantages of moving to a better location and decided it's worth more to me to live here. I've lived here for five or six years and never got into any unnecessary trouble. It suits my purposes perfectly.[19]

For this reason the situations involving nondeviants examined in this section had mostly superficial meaning to the professionals. Many (though fewer than the nonprofessionals) could think of one or more instances in their nonprison past where they had been in such situations, but these were not recurrent features of their daily lives as they were for the nonprofessionals. Even here the transactions with nondeviants were not disliked as often as was the case for the nonprofessionals; thus, they were not so frequently interpreted as penalties.

The Renunciation Social Penalties

The evidence from the present study and other research permits us to suggest the following as hypothetical perceived renunciation social penalties:

6. Being questioned by casual acquaintances about aspects of one's criminal life is an unsettling experience for the nonprofessional criminal.

7. Curiosity and recognition stares at the nonprofessional criminal by nondeviant members of the community are odious to him.

8. Where the nonprofessional criminal is known, he will experience direct insults to his face and audibly and intentionally behind his back.

9. For the nonprofessional criminal, a deviant who regards his identity as degrading, the shame and embarrassment associated with the early weeks of release from prison are renunciation social penalties.

10. The nonprofessional criminal is apprehensive about the treatment to be accorded him when he is forced to interact with those with whom he is only very casually acquainted but who know of his prison record.

All these penalties depend upon an awareness of the ex-offender's criminal record by the others in the interactive situation. Such awareness, in turn, depends upon many factors, such as the notoriety of his specific case or cases, the size of the community, the efficiency of the communications media, the seriousness of the offense or offenses, and so forth. All these variables affect a deviant's chances of avoiding the penalties listed above. We have not systematically examined each of these factors in the present study since they are beyond its scope; they constitute a separate research project of their own. However, some data were collected on the size of communities from which the nonprofessionals came, as well as on their notoriety within those communities. The distribution of respondents by size of community is presented below in Table 4.

TABLE 4

DISTRIBUTION OF NONPROFESSIONALS
BY SIZE OF COMMUNITY, 1961

COMMUNITY SIZE	Number	Percent
Under 250	2	8.7
250–999	3	13.0
1,000–2,499	2	8.7
2,500–4,999	1	4.4
5,000–7,499	2	8.7
Corner Brook (25,185)	6	26.1
St. John's (63,633)	7	30.4
Totals	23*	100.0

* One respondent lived in two different communities during the course of his criminal career.

The ten men who lived in communities with populations of less than 7,499 were known for their criminal deeds throughout the community, with the exception of one who had only recently moved into his place of residence. Many of these reported that their reputation had spread beyond their hometown to neighboring villages. Of the thirteen respondents who lived in the island's two cities, 39 percent felt that their name as a criminal had spread beyond their neighborhood to others in the same community. One of these men also claimed facial recognition beyond his immediate neighborhood, a fact which was obviously true since one of his crimes had been covered extensively in the local mass media.

The professionals adopted a different strategy for coping with the problem of community notoriety: for this reason and others they simply relocated themselves in large cities or kept constantly on the move. Most of them were raised, however, in communities of less than 100,000 people.

One further mode of identification which came to the interviewer's attention during the course of the study is that of prison tattoos. To the author's knowledge, no one has looked at this practice as a way of unwittingly labeling oneself as a deviant for the larger community.[20] All the respondents in the present study as well as selected prison officials agreed that they could easily tell a prison tattoo from a professional one, and that this knowledge was not limited only to those who had been in penal institutions. It also had some generality in lower-class neighborhoods and possibly among the police. Apparently the distinguishing features of prison tattoos are their unartistic characteristics: the tattoo lines are often crooked, these lines blur with time, and the skin is often reddish and swollen around the tattoo. These qualities stem from the inferior tattooing equipment and the lack of skill in using it. How widely and effectively a prison tattoo, as distinguished from a professional or another amateur tattoo, identifies an individual as an ex-offender is a question worth considering in future theorizing and research.[21]

INTERPERSONAL RELATIONS IN PASSING

Erving Goffman has discussed at length the problems (for us, the penalties) of deviants who "pass" or enter into encounters with nondeviants who do not know their true identity and who therefore accept them as nondeviants. As Goffman points out, such a practice opens up for the passing person the chance of experiencing many unsettling events.[22]

One of these events is the possibility that the deviant will meet unanticipated needs to disclose discrediting information about himself. Sixty-eight percent of the respondents admitted being in at least one social situation where they were forced to talk about their criminal life in some way. Usually this happened in innocent question-asking by the other parties present, such as "how come you weren't around last year when so-and-so was running for election?" As far as the respondents knew, people making these inquiries were unaware of their prison background; the questions being asked were common and legitimate for the content of daily conversation. Under these circumstances the nonprofessional felt he had little choice but to admit his deviant record, since to manufacture a plausible but face-saving story on the spot meant running the risk of triggering further conversation along those lines and eventual discovery anyway. Some of the typical reactions to these situations are presented below:

> One guy asked me what I was doing awhile back, and how I happened to know another fellow who was also an ex-con. I simply told him the truth, but I felt sick about it—I got this lump in my throat.

> This girl asked me how long I had been with the circus— I just couldn't avoid telling her of my record. She also knew a friend of mine who had been in.

> A fellow asked me how I enjoyed my summer. I took this as an insult, but the ——— kept asking questions. I tried to change the subject, and finally he quit.

> Oh, that happened a lot to me at work. I never told them a thing. I tried to avoid giving them a chance to ask questions. When they did I told them I was fishing. If you tell them the truth, they'd ask more questions, and I don't like that.

The nonprofessional criminal may also be forced to disclose information about his past if someone who knows of his record comes along when he is with others who do not know of it. Many in the Newfoundland sample reported that this too had happened to them. No matter how the respondent was forced to reveal his criminal past to relative strangers, he did not like it. Eighty percent of the sample reported that situations like this upset them, and led them to adopt such tactics as trying to change the subject or even leaving the situation. However, the men most commonly reported that they simply remained, gritted their teeth, and answered the questions in such a way that it was obvious they did not wish to talk any more than necessary about that matter. A small proportion, 26 percent, even reported that they had avoided making close friends for this reason. The following are representative instances of this sort of transaction between deviants and nondeviants:

> I was on a boat where a fellow from home joined the crew. I guess he didn't know for sure that I had been in prison so he asked me in front of some of the others. I didn't like it, but I had to give him an answer.

> Yes, that has happened to me a couple of times. I got shook up—upset—I let it come, but tried to stop any more questions or conversations on that subject.

> Someone came along at a dance once. I hated it. If a chap does it as a joke, I get mad. I have left the place a couple of times.

> You get nervous because you don't know what to do: whether to reveal or not to reveal your record.

> Somebody did come along once who knew of my record. I thought they were going to say something. I feel nervous when these things happen. I've often left before questions could come from the fellow that knew.

Of the remaining 32 percent who said they had never been in such circumstances, half of them were not even aware that such a thing could happen. It is, of course, possible in small-town living that since everyone knows about an ex-offender's past history there would be no opportunity to talk about his criminal record in the way being discussed here. With respect to the residual 20 percent who reported that they did not object to such encounters, we might speculate, as before, that this is evidence that these individuals were developing into adjusted pathological deviants.

In reaction to this and similar situations, the deviant may develop adaptive techniques that unwittingly give rise to hurt feelings and misunderstandings on the part of others present. For example, he may get angry when others in the setting, in all innocence, start asking questions about his past for some ordinarily acceptable reason. He may reply in a sarcastic manner to a naïve observation made by someone present about criminal behavior, an observation stimulated by, say, a recent notorious bank holdup. The ex-inmate involved may attempt to adjust by abruptly changing the subject, thereby confusing the others and interrupting the normal flow of conversation. It would seem plausible to consider this set of circumstances as a renunciation social penalty since the deviant with the proper amount of empathy for the feelings of others would himself feel somewhat remorseful for having upset them. Further, the whole problem could be avoided if he just stayed away from conventional surroundings.

The evidence from the present study does not support this last assertion very strongly. Only 30 percent of the nonprofessionals interviewed claimed to have been aware of hurting others' feelings in this way, although all of these reported feeling sorry and upset in retrospect about having done so. It is possible, as we have suggested earlier, that the role-taking ability of many of these ex-offenders is not well developed, an observation leading us to suggest that until this factor is controlled in investigation we will not gain any definitive information about this potential penalty. However, even if we should discover that with the proper level of role-taking ability ex-offenders do find such situations upsetting for themselves as well as for others, this would be a penalty only to some ex-offenders. As a social penalty it will always be limited to those with adequately developed empathic processes, a possession which seems to vary among people everywhere.[23]

Another possible renunciation social penalty stems from the fact that those who pass learn the often humiliating truth about what nondeviant others think about people like themselves. Seventy percent of the Newfoundland sample reported hearing negative remarks about criminals in such contexts and, of these, 86 percent said they were disturbed by the remarks. The usual reaction to such situations, as to many of the others discussed so far, was to stay and take it. Some, however, claimed they argued with those making the humiliating statements in spite of the obvious threats to the secrecy of their own deviant identity. Other strategies were to leave the situation, get mad at the person making the remarks, try to change the subject, and in a couple of cases to confront the others with the fact of their deviant record. It is evident that in reacting to this social penalty, the ex-offender puts himself in a position to be penalized again by hurting the feelings of others in the encounter.

The remarks heard were anything but complimentary, and were usually about another ex-offender or an act of criminality recently reported in the mass media. The respondents in this study admitted hearing statements like: "He must have been half a fool to go in there" (the store held up). "Don't go around with him." "He should have been shot." "They should keep them in there" (prison). "They're a bunch of gangsters down there" (Her Majesty's Penitentiary in St. John's). Mr. Frank P. Miller, Executive Director of the National Parole Service in Canada, reports the following case history:

A few years ago a laughing happy group of six University students—three men and three girls—sat in a restaurant. They were enjoying conversation and an after theatre snack.

The girls started some woman talk—if you like. The men got on to sports. One of the men was a little older than the other two. But this was not unusual at that time; the Universities still had "veteran" students. He listened to his friends' talk about the goal that was missed. The girls' conversation was simply a buzz in his ear. He had a sense of well-being in this company.

Suddenly, what seemed to him to be loud and clear was the voice of the girl next to him (actually she hadn't changed the tone of her voice) as she said, "I wouldn't be seen dead with an ex-convict." Almost in panic, he managed to murmur excuses and apologies and got out. He was an ex-convict.

He was not a first offender—nor just a mixed-up kid who had got into bad company. He had not just spent a few months in the reformatory. He was on parole—on a long sentence—and I mean a long sentence—and it was not the first sentence—not just the second nor even the third. From about age fourteen he had built himself a considerable criminal career. His offences were not limited to petty shoplifting. He was an armed robber.[24]

The professionals reacted somewhat differently to these remarks. They often saw them as inaccurate and, although it depended upon the nature of the situation, they would frequently make an effort to correct the thinking of the others present. That their deviant status might have been discovered in the process did not seem to worry the professionals who, as we shall note shortly, felt so well in control of the interaction that they could prevent this from happening. Of course it is possible that the more limited contact with nondeviants experienced by this group of respondents affected their strategies for handling these matters. If the situation did not call for remonstration, they were likely simply to remain silent on the issue at hand; it was not considered desirable to get angry, to try to change the subject, or to leave the encounter.

There is another possible social penalty closely related to some of those already presented in this section: he who passes is never sure whether someone in the situation does not have information about his identity. This set of circumstances is penalizing in that there is always some degree of anxiety about encounters with casual acquaintances which would not exist if the ex-offender had not ventured outside sympathetic social circles. There seem to be two issues involved here. First, there is the question for the ex-offender of whether the others in the encounter know of his record. If he thinks they do not know, then he may try to keep it secret; whereas if he thinks they do know, then a different strategy is called for, such as restricting conversation to areas believed to be "safe" or indicating openly that he does not wish to discuss the matter. Until he can define those present as being either aware or unaware of his past, his subsequent behavior is likely to be hesitant and experimental as he attempts to learn the actual state of their knowledge about him. Or, he may, given the nature of the company, simply assume one or the other and act accordingly. Second, once some or all of those present have been identified as people who do know of his record, the deviant wonders just how much they know. Do they know how long he was behind bars? Do they know the nature of his crime? Do they know the extenuating circumstances which he thinks must be considered in judging him? Again, under certain conditions action may be greatly impeded until more accurate information about the state of knowledge of the others in the setting is obtained.

More than 68 percent of the Newfoundland sample reported that they had been in interactive situations where
they thought their prison record was not known but where
it turned out that someone present did, in fact, possess that
information. Eighty percent of these expressed dislike for
such surprises, the usual reaction being to stay there and make
the best of things as they had developed. In a small minority
of these instances, the respondent remained in the situation
but refused to discuss his past. The other 20 percent who
had at least one such experience did not express dislike; they
seemed, as before, to be reacting to commitment by becoming adjusted to their deviant identity.

The fact that 32 percent of the total number of respondents had not had such an experience is not surprising in
view of the intimate surroundings of the small rural communities from which almost half of them came. Nevertheless,
only one of the twenty-two men interviewed said that he was
not aware that such a thing could happen. That this is a salient
renunciation social penalty for the nonprofessional criminal
is emphasized by the fact that half of the respondents in the
present study reported that they had avoided social relations
with nondeviant others for this reason.

As we indicated earlier, the professional had only limited contact with nondeviants although this contact did involve a certain amount of passing. But since his major goals
did not usually depend upon his ability to dissimulate as a
conventional member of the community, what interchanges
he had with people in this walk of life were not, as a rule,
tense events. Indeed, the professional showed little fear of
those situations where he did not wish to be identified as
deviant, where potentially he could be exposed as an imposter
and certain of his intentions embarrassed. Under these cir-

cumstances most of the respondents reported, often proudly, of being able to manufacture a plausible story which delivered them from any impending difficulties. Rather than being penalizing, these situations seemed to be perceived as sport, a chance to utilize certain social skills associated with professional crime under conditions of minimum risk.[25]

The Renunciation Social Penalties

On the basis of the data gathered in the present study, the following perceived renunciation social penalties are suggested as receiving tentative support:

11. While passing, the nonprofessional criminal meets unanticipated needs to disclose discrediting information about himself.
12. While passing, the nonprofessional criminal opens himself up to the opportunity of hearing the often humiliating truth about how nondeviant others view people like himself.
13. In attempting to pass, the nonprofessional criminal is never sure whether someone in the situation does not have information about his deviant past.

Each of these penalties is seen as arising out of the deviant's attempts to interact with conventional members of the community while keeping his deviant identity secret—i.e., while attempting to pass. They function as commitment-generating penalties by demonstrating to the individual that he would not have experienced them if he had interacted only with sympathetic others, usually other deviants.

So far in this chapter we have concentrated upon interpersonal relations in ongoing social situations where the deviant's criminal record is known to others present or where it is unknown and he is attempting to pass. From the pioneering work of Erving Goffman in this area and from the data gathered in the present study, we have isolated several renunciation social penalties for the nonprofessional criminal (Numbers 6 through 13).

Whether or not events in any one social situation are perceived by the deviant as penalizing depends upon his definition of that situation. The definition of the situation is a personal interrelation and interpretation of the social, psychological, physiological, and physical elements present in the setting.[26] Thus, whether a situation is penalizing or potentially penalizing depends upon, for example, who is in it. Many of the respondents reported that they were more anxious about passing and its attendant surprises when they were at a dance hall trying to impress a particular girl. The definition of the situation depends upon the attitudes which the deviant brings to the situation. We have seen so far that most of the nonprofessional criminals interviewed regard their deviant identity as degrading while a small proportion seem to have become adjusted to it. These attitudes toward themselves influenced their interpretation of the events in the situations discussed in the interviews—most being upset, but a few not being bothered at all. The setting itself would appear to be important, as in the example above where passing in a dance hall arouses greater anxiety than, say, passing in a certain kind of tavern.

Basically, then, we have been engaged so far in this chapter in studying the nonprofessional ex-offender's definition of certain situations and some of his subsequent reactions to those situations. We are asserting that on the basis of such definitions, which describe many different kinds of situations, both deviant and nondeviant, as penalizing and unsettling, the deviant will retrospectively conclude that life is, on the balance, more satisfying outside the conventional world. In doing so he also recognizes that he is committed to deviance.

THE LACK OF UNDERSTANDING AS A SOCIAL PENALTY

In this section we are interested less in specific definitions of particular situations than in the general attitudes that develop out of many such definitions. As the deviant interacts with members of the conventional world, he comes to learn more vividly than ever their sentiments about people similar to himself. Some, if not most of these views are in some way distorted. In this respect Lemert has noticed that when deviance and the attitudinal responses of different segments of the community are mediated by a chain of formal relationships, the societal reaction may be exaggerated or in some other way distorted. Such deviance he calls "putative deviance." [27] Elsewhere he goes on to note that when putative definitions persist over a period of time stereotypes of that form of deviance develop.[28] Such a situation cuts down the effectiveness of the role-taking of nondeviants when applied to deviants in the community, and eventually leads to further deviance.[29]

The respondents in the present study were questioned as to whether they thought members of the conventional world understood the problems ex-offenders experienced when they tried to abandon their deviant identity. The results are presented below in Table 5. Almost 64 percent of the nonprofessionals felt that nondeviants lacked under-

TABLE 5

NONPROFESSIONALS' PERCEPTION OF NONDEVIANTS' UNDERSTANDING OF THEIR PROBLEMS

AMOUNT OF UNDERSTANDING	Number	Percent
Nondeviants have understanding	4	18.2
Nondeviants have some understanding	5	22.7
Nondeviants have no understanding	9	40.9
Don't know	4	18.2
Totals	22	100.0

standing to a greater or lesser degree. Perhaps this figure would have been higher had more of the interviewees been residents of Corner Brook or St. John's since, as Wilkins points out, the larger communities prevent accurate information about deviants from spreading because of a lack of firsthand contact with them.[30] It is instructive to note, in this regard, that 79 percent of the professionals who, as a group, were more urbanized, felt that nondeviants lacked understanding.

Although the proportion of "don't know" answers indicates caution, on the basis of this evidence we are tentatively suggesting lack of understanding as a renunciation social penalty:

14. A perceived lack of understanding of the nonprofessional criminal's problems is a renunciation social penalty.

A low degree of understanding in the nondeviant sphere of life is seen by the nonprofessional criminal as penalizing when compared with the relatively higher degrees of sympathy encountered among other deviants.

NOTES

1. Continuance commitment does not mean that the deviant individual is restricted in his interaction only to similar deviants. The circle of association includes those who are sympathetic to his plight, such as certain other types of deviants (a jazz musician will accept a homosexual, for example), certain classes of nondeviants, and possibly even social workers or the police who are considered to be "wise."

2. Louis Zeitoun, "Parole Supervision and Self-Determination," *Federal Probation* 26 (September 1962): 1–4.

3. Erving Goffman, *Stigma: Notes on the Management of Spoiled Identity,* pp. 12–13. As the reader will soon see, the intellectual debt to Goffman throughout this chapter and the next is considerable.

4. Goffman has observed that this is a characteristic of all who are stigmatized (ibid., p. 16).

5. This practice, at least in the past, frequently has been found among jazz musicians and is known by them as "putting-on," "farting-off," or some equivalent expression.

6. Goffman, *Stigma,* p. 18.

7. Trasler emphasizes that social skills, such as role-taking ability, generally decline with repeated and sustained incarcera-

tion. See Gordon Trasler, "The Social Relations of Persistent Offenders," *The Sociological Review Monograph, No. 9: Sociological Studies in the British Penal Services,* ed. Paul Halmos, p. 94.

8. Goffman, *Stigma,* p. 16.

9. Erving Goffman, *Behavior in Public Places,* p. 84.

10. Clifford R. Shaw, *The Jack Roller,* p. 116.

11. Ibid., p. 118.

12. Trasler, "Social Relations," p. 94.

13. A. M. Kirkpatrick, "The Human Problems of Prison After-Care," rev. ed., p. 6.

14. A. M. Kirkpatrick, "After-Care and the Prisoner's Aid Societies," in *Crime and Its Treatment in Canada,* ed. William T. McGrath, p. 397; Trasler, "Social Relations," p. 84.

15. Trasler, "Social Relations," pp. 94–95.

16. Daniel Glaser, *The Effectiveness of a Prison and Parole System,* pp. 392–393, 541.

17. Goffman, *Stigma,* p. 13.

18. Ibid., pp. 14–15.

19. John Bartlow Martin, ed., *My Life in Crime,* p. 269.

20. A few authors have discussed other identifying functions of the tattoo, such as gang membership. See John H. Burma, "Self-Tattooing among Delinquents," *Sociology and Social Research* 43 (May–June 1959): 343–344; Herbert Bloch and Arthur Niederhoffer, *The Gang.*

21. For the interested it is also worth noting that many of those nonprofessionals interviewed had tattooed dice and other patterns of four and five round dots on their hands and fingers. Again, most inmates and prison officials seemed to agree that these dots stood for the following expressions, respectively: "we will work today" (4 Ws), and "we won't work will we" (5 Ws). When asked if in the Newfoundland prison system these had any meaning in terms of presence or absence of inmate cooperation, officials said it did not. Our interest, however, focuses on the potential which these figures have for identification of the deviant by informed nondeviants.

22. All the penalties discussed in this section have been de-

rived from Goffman's thoughts on passing. See Goffman, *Stigma*, pp. 83–86.

23. Both Stryker and Kinch suggest some of the ways in which role-taking ability can vary among people. See Sheldon Stryker, "Conditions of Accurate Role-Taking: A Test of Mead's Theory," in *Human Behavior and Social Processes,* ed. Arnold M. Rose, pp. 41–62; John W. Kinch, "A Formalized Theory of The Self-Concept," *American Journal of Sociology* 68 (January 1963): 481–486. Although he does not put it in these terms, Newcomb provides evidence for variation in role-taking ability in the development of interpersonal relationships. Theodore M. Newcomb, *The Acquaintance Process,* chap. 6.

24. Frank P. Miller, "Parole and The Community" (Address delivered at the Annual Meeting of the John Howard Society of Windsor, Ontario, February 1961).

25. Whether or not our professionals actually possessed this ability to talk their way out of potentially embarrassing encounters with nondeviants is a moot question. Such skill is usually most likely to be found among professional thieves: swindlers, pickpockets, hotel prowlers, and the like. There is a chance that what the interviewer observed here was an expression of the respondent's ideal self, rather than the self as typically manifested. The professional thief, partly because of his glibness, enjoys considerable prestige in the underworld, perhaps even more than the professional "heavy" criminal. See Don C. Gibbons, *Society, Crime, and Criminal Careers,* pp. 245–257.

26. Robert A. Stebbins, "A Theory of the Definition of the Situation," *The Canadian Review of Sociology and Anthropology* 4 (August 1967): 156–158; "Studying the Definition of the Situation: Theory and Field Research Strategies," *The Canadian Review of Sociology and Anthropology* 6 (November 1969): 193–211. A further discussion of the interrelationship of these variables is available here.

27. Edwin M. Lemert, *Social Pathology,* pp. 55–56. An example of a chain of formal relationships through which information about the deviant is passed is that of arresting officer to police chief to newspaper reporter to editor.

28. Ibid., p. 64. See also J. L. Simmons, "Public Stereotypes of Deviants," *Social Problems* 13 (Fall 1965): 223–232.

29. A similar model has been proposed by Wilkins. Our objections to this one are that it does not allow for obvious facts like the deviant successfully integrating himself into conventional life or the selecting of any of the various other alternatives available to one committed in a self-degrading way. See Leslie T. Wilkins, *Social Deviance: Social Policy, Action, and Research,* chap. 4.

30. Ibid., p. 85. It should be clear that we are talking about understanding and not tolerance. A small community promotes a great deal of understanding by permitting firsthand contact, but the opposite is often true for tolerance. On the other hand, larger communities promote considerable tolerance, but foster a low degree of understanding.

6

RENUNCIATION
SOCIAL PENALTIES IN
INTERPERSONAL
LIFE, II

In this chapter we shift our emphasis from social situations in general to those involving specific categories of actors; the police, relatives, friends, single women, and wives. Treatment by each of these groups of people can be penalizing to the extent of creating the feeling of commitment to a deviant identity.

INTERPERSONAL RELATIONS
WITH THE POLICE

Glaser's study disclosed that men come out of prison with fears of police harassment, fears presumably learned from the inmate culture.[1] Yet these sentiments notwithstanding, Glaser was able to conclude that "despite the dramatic accounts of a few instances of alleged extreme injustice, the total number of cases in which a serious police harassment problem was indicated by the subject's account or the probation office record amount to only 6 per cent of the successful releases and 8 per cent of the returned violators." His data suggest that "where the police were suspicious of felony behavior there was likely to be a basis for their suspicion, and other types of police action had no serious implications." [2] Nevertheless, this apparently varies some by police jurisdictions.

With a couple of possible exceptions, there is no evidence in the present study of harassment by the police amounting to anything more than routine questioning about crimes in which, from their standpoint, the ex-offender had some chance of being involved. As far as the interviewer could tell, no physical assault occurred in these encounters with the police, again with a few exceptions.

As long as police contact maintains this level of interaction, there would appear to be little about it that is penalizing, and if it were penalizing, it would most certainly be as a continuation social penalty. All the ex-offender would have to do is to remain free from crime and other criminals for a long enough period of time, and these contacts would cease. However, it should be added that there is always the possibility of a boomerang effect, in which increasing resentment at these practices leads to an "I'll-show-them" attitude. Perhaps this accounts for the 6 to 8 percent who experienced harassment in Glaser's samples.

There is another way, however, in which police contact with a potential suspect can be considered a renunciation social penalty. It has less to do with the fact of contact and questioning than with the manner in which it is carried out.

More specifically, police surveillance, when it is done in the view of or with the knowledge of some or all of the non-deviant members of the community, can embarrass the ex-offender's position by publicizing this deviance and the possibility that he has not yet reformed. Furthermore, attractive friends, relatives, and employers, all of whom are "straight," may be upset over the appearance of the police at their homes or places of work because of the questions such activity might raise among important peers in the neighborhood. For the deviant who is trying to reestablish himself within conventional circles, real or potential contact by the police can cause considerable anxiety. This stress would not exist if he were not trying to abandon his deviant identity, since he would not care how the contact disturbed his image with nondeviants. In that case, the only penalty possible would be the chance of painful physical or mental treatment, which appears to be small.

It was this public kind of police contact which upset the twenty-two nonprofessional respondents in the present study, and there are many ways in which it was done. Half of the respondents reported that the police contacted them at least once in uniform and a marked police car instead of in plain clothes and an unmarked car. Somewhat over 50 percent claimed that they were picked up or questioned on the street or in a public place, such as a tavern, restaurant, ball park, etc. Many reported that they were contacted at work, which in some instances forced them to reveal their criminal record to their employers. In half of these cases the respondent stated that his employer was upset over the event, apparently over the fact that the police had made an appearance in his establishment. The most common place of contact was the ex-offender's home, but even this brought repercussions in that parents and wives objected to the image projected to the neighborhood when the police came to the house. Comments by the nonprofessionals illustrate these sentiments.

> I don't like it. I get mad and tell them off. Every time I see a police car I get a lump in my throat, a pit in my stomach—my heart pounds. There is always the possibility of a false rap.

> I get mad at them—tell them right there that I don't like being nailed with friends.

> It hurts my feelings that they suspect me. I don't get mad at them to their face.

> I get mad, but I cooperate. It disrupts our fishing activities until the questioning is done—I have to go to another town for this.

> I don't like it at all—tell them I know nothing about it. They treat me pretty well though.

> I was dragged into their car off the street once. Another time I was stopped at the ball park. I get mad and tell them off—I would like to kill them. Often I run when I see them coming.

> It gets me mad when they come to the house—gives father a bad name.

How much can be done about this is a moot question, since the police must do their job. The fact that all of the nonprofessional respondents were third- and fourth-time offenders indicates that official suspicion was not without foundation. But whether this sort of approach to contacting suspects is good or bad, inevitable or not, one thing is certain: it angered the ex-offenders.[3] As we have just seen, the specific reactions varied. Many reported getting a lump in their throats despite the fact that they knew they had done nothing that time. Some said that even the sight of a police car made them extremely uneasy.

However, it also turned out that a majority of the professionals became angry when contacted in this fashion by the police. If anger in this situation is related strictly to the problems such interchanges cause for men trying to reestablish themselves in conventional society, as we just suggested for the nonprofessionals, then our finding is paradoxical. On the other hand, if anger on the part of the professionals is an expression of resentment at this invasion of privacy or of a sort of righteous indignation, then this poses no threat to our theory. Unfortunately, there is no evidence from this study that can help us interpret these results. Nevertheless, it is of interest that a minority (six professionals) were not upset by police surveillance; they simply regarded such activities as part of routine police work.

With these reservations it would still seem that there is sufficient evidence from the present study to hypothesize the following perceived renunciation social penalty:

15. For the nonprofessional criminal trying to reestablish himself in the conventional world, contact with police who suspect him of a crime can potentially publicize his deviance and make him anxious about his reception in the community.

INTERPERSONAL RELATIONS
WITH FRIENDS AND RELATIVES

Both Goffman and Lemert have suggested that to the degree the deviant is recognized by the individual members of the community and to the degree these nondeviants believe that his stigma will generalize to them if they associate with him, they will establish the necessary amount of social distance to prevent this.[4] It is logical to suppose that this proposition might be applied to family relations and to relations with male and female friends; and it includes the possibility of severing or, with friends, preventing a relationship from being established.

The respondents in the present study were interviewed along these lines. As far as male friends were concerned, there was apparently little change from the period before the person went to prison; over 90 percent of the nonprofessionals replied that they were treated the same as, and in a few cases even better than, before they were convicted. They did admit that many of their friends appeared awkward when they were first released, but that this did not last.

Presumably, much of this depends upon how worried one's friends are about their own reputation. In this connection it is instructive to note that a vast majority of the respondents had at least some friends who themselves had been in prison (see Table 6). Furthermore, in over 68 percent of the cases all of the respondents' friends knew of their prison records and another 23 percent reported that only a few friends were ignorant of the fact. Thus, one cannot attribute the continued acceptance of the ex-offender by his friends to

TABLE 6

NUMBER OF MALE FRIENDS WHO HAD BEEN
IN PRISON (NONPROFESSIONALS ONLY)

NUMBER OF FRIENDS	Number	Percent
None	2	9.1
A few	8	36.4
About half	5	22.7
Most	7	31.8
Totals	22	100.0

the fact that the latter were unaware of the former's true identity. Approximately these same results were found among the professionals, except that they had considerably fewer nondeviant friends.

That Glaser's findings were roughly the same in his more extensive survey in the United States leads us to the conclusion that so far there is no sufficient evidence to warrant labeling rejection by friends as a renunciation social penalty [5]—at least not until the variable of the friends' reputations is more adequately controlled.

Approximately the same thing can be said for interpersonal relations with female friends. Eighty-five percent of the nonprofessional and professional respondents replied that female companions in general treated them as well after prison as before. However, almost half of the nonprofessional sample reported at least one instance of being rejected because of their prison records, while one-third of the professionals mentioned such an experience. As in the case of male friends, much seems to depend upon how female friends view the effects of such an association on their own reputation. It is possible that females in general will be found to be more sensitive than males to the threat of contagion of the deviant's stigma, and that they will therefore be less likely to associate with such people.

Even relations with the family of orientation did not deteriorate for a majority of those interviewed, another finding which seems to be congruent with Glaser.[6] Sixty-eight percent of the nonprofessionals and 52 percent of the professionals replied that all of their kin treated them as well after their imprisonment as before. Only 27 percent of those in Newfoundland (and 48 percent of those in Dorchester) said that some of their relatives (mostly parents) treated them worse than before their convictions, while a few interviewees claimed complete rejection by their families. As with their male friends, all or nearly all of the ex-offenders' close relatives knew of their deviant behavior and their prison terms.[7]

Although evidence from the present study and from other research does not support the hypothesis that rejection by male and female friends and by one's family is penalizing (because such rejection does not seem to occur), the family life of ex-offenders may have at least one other undesirable aspect. A man may be accepted into his family of orientation upon release from prison, but his acts of deviance may have lost him the respect of these significant others. Comments by some of the respondents in the Newfoundland sample indicate that the resulting shame might well be a penalty.[8] At first glance it seems that such a penalty could function either as a renunciation penalty ("If I weren't trying to reform I wouldn't be with these people") or as a continuation penalty

("If I would stay out of trouble I would have more respect").
Further research is needed to determine which of these penalties is experienced by which classes of nonprofessional
criminals.

CHANGES IN INTERPERSONAL RELATIONSHIPS

The content of interpersonal relationships undergoes change
as soon as the two people involved are separated from each
other. Lengthy separation would seem then to engender even
greater change in the parties. Alfred Schutz has stated the
matter in the following way:

> I know that my fellowman has grown older since he left
> me, and upon reflection, I know that, strictly speaking, he
> has changed with each additional experience, with each
> new situation. But all this I fail to take into account in the
> routine of everyday life. I hold on to the familiar image I
> have of you. I take it for granted that you are as I have
> known you before. Until further notice I hold invariant
> that segment of my stock of knowledge which concerns
> you and which I have built up in face-to-face situations,
> that is, until I receive information to the contrary.[9]

Not only do interpersonal relationships undergo change
when the actors are separately having new experiences, but
when the interval is a long one the degree of intimacy is
attenuated. Even when the relationship is maintained by
letters and similar devices, each party addresses himself only
to a typification of the other person as he knew him before

he departed.[10] Since each person is changing in the other's absence, it is impossible to maintain the same degree of reliable knowledge as is found in more or less continual face-to-face relations.

All of this is seen here as potentially penalizing to the ex-offender who has returned from serving a prison sentence. People are not the same as they were before and, of course, neither is he. However, the penalty is a continuation social penalty since it would not have occurred if the person in question's deviant behavior had not been discovered, and it will not recur if he does not deviate again.

Somewhat more than 45 percent of the nonprofessional respondents in the present study reported that they had noticed evidence of personality change in their friends and relatives, including such changes as those resulting from marriage, new interests, greater maturity, steady employment, and so forth. Theoretically, we would have expected a greater number to have admitted such changes, but again it must be emphasized that many of the prison sentences were short, and perhaps the actual personality transformations in significant others were too subtle to be perceived by the ex-offenders. The length of incarceration does apparently make a difference since the professionals all reported noticing changes. Much would depend, too, upon how sensitive the individual is to these matters. It is possible that the period of uneasiness just after release from prison is partly caused by a barely detectable strangeness between formerly close friends and relatives, a strangeness that dissipates with adjustment to slightly changed personalities.

More significant, however, is the finding that those nonprofessionals and professionals who did perceive changes in their friends and relatives did not interpret them as penalizing: they reported they still felt nearly as close to them. Over 90 percent of the Newfoundland respondents claimed that they knew these people as well after their release as before they were incarcerated. The same proportion reported that they felt no hesitation about asking formerly close friends and relatives for favors in the same ways as they would have before prison. Yet exactly 50 percent reported that they had lost contact with certain significant others, most of whom had moved away to the mainland or, as in a few cases, had died. In three instances contact simply was never renewed. The professional's position on these matters, as might be expected, was inconclusive. He had far fewer "square" friends to lose contact with, experience distance from, or ask favors of. Underworld friends posed no problem in this regard.

In light of the reservations expressed above, it is only reasonable to conclude that the evidence from our respondents is not comprehensive enough to rule out changes in the personalities of significant others as a possible continuation social penalty. More subtle questions and other measuring techniques must be devised, and the researcher must be alert to the possibility that even if such changes are perceived as being penalizing immediately upon release from prison, they may not always be so interpreted. Intimate face-to-face relations can be reestablished, perhaps rather quickly.[11]

RESPONSIBILITY IN
FAMILY AFFAIRS

We dealt to some extent with the question of responsibility when we reported our findings and those of others on such matters as work habits. In this section we will examine responsibility in strictly family matters, such as child rearing and decision making.

It has been suggested that it is difficult for the returning ex-offender to assume a role of responsibility in his family of procreation. For one thing the wife, who has of necessity gained the degree of independence needed to maintain the family alone, may be reluctant to give it up, a fact which may threaten the role of the husband.[12] On the other hand, the disposition to make responsible decisions may have been badly undermined by the dependency-creating ways of institutional life. Finally, a totally male existence of the kind encountered in the average prison would seem to make matters like disciplining and raising children very foreign and distasteful to a released offender.[13]

It is here suggested that being forced into a family role of responsibility can be considered a renunciation social penalty, a cost the ex-offender must endure if he is going to associate with family members who demand that he perform his family roles in the traditional ways of the community. He may find that making decisions, disciplining children, and trying to find and hold a job so that those dependent upon him are provided for are a strange set of requirements, one for which he has little liking.[14] The nonprofessional criminal at this stage of his deviant career reasons that these demands would not be made upon him if he had remained in his deviant identity and dismissed family responsibilities as a problem for his wife.[15]

Questions to gather data on these issues were designed for the present study. Unfortunately, only two of the twenty-two nonprofessional interviewees had any family to be responsible for, and only one of these men had any children. The situation was exactly the same for the professional respondents. Verification of this hypothesized renunciation social penalty depends upon the findings of future research. Whatever these findings may be, they will only apply to a minority of the criminal population since, according to the best evidence available, only 30 to 40 percent of these deviants are married.[16] How many of these have children appears still to be an open question. Perhaps they reason as John Martin did:

> But I never felt that I was in a position to get married. It isn't fair. You see, after you've got a record, after you've been in trouble, you get married say, and that stuff comes bouncing back at you. You're making other people suffer for things they're not responsible for. When you've got a sheet, it's just the same as going around with a cement sack on your shoulder, it's a burden you got to carry. It's nobody's fault but your own. But it's there, you got it.[17]

SUMMARY AND CONCLUSIONS

Evidence from the present study, with occasional supplementary data from other investigations, presented in the last two chapters enables us to advance the following as hypothetical perceived renunciation social penalties:

6. Being questioned by casual acquaintances about aspects of one's criminal life is an unsettling experience for the nonprofessional criminal.

7. Curiosity and recognition stares at the nonprofessional criminal by nondeviant members of the community are odious to him.

8. Where the nonprofessional criminal is known, he will experience direct insults to his face and audibly and intentionally behind his back.

9. For the nonprofessional criminal, a deviant who regards his identity as degrading, the shame and embarrassment associated with the early weeks of release from prison are a renunciation social penalty.

10. The nonprofessional criminal is apprehensive about the treatment to be accorded him when he is forced to interact with those with whom he is only very casually acquainted but who know of his prison record.

11. While passing, the nonprofessional criminal meets unanticipated needs to disclose discrediting information about himself.

12. While passing, the nonprofessional criminal opens himself up to the opportunity of hearing the often humiliating truth about how nondeviant others view people like himself.

13. In attempting to pass, the nonprofessional criminal is never sure whether someone in the situation does not have information about his deviant past, which is perceived as a renunciation social penalty.

14. A perceived lack of understanding by nondeviants of the nonprofessional criminal's problems engendered when he tries to abandon his deviant identity is a renunciation social penalty.

15. For the nonprofessional criminal trying to reestablish himself in the conventional world, contact with police who suspect him of a crime can potentially publicize his deviance and make him anxious about his reception in the community.

Each of these is seen as penalizing because the individual would not have experienced the penalty if he chose to remain in his deviant identity and associate only with other deviants and persons sympathetic to his situation. These renunciation social penalties are different from those presented in Chapter 4 in that they restrict interpersonal relations to contacts with sympathetic others, while those focusing on the deviant's material life restrict the opportunities related to earning a living to those possible in full or partial criminality or at best in some marginal activity.

Penalties 6 through 9 exist for the deviant because his criminal identity is known to those with whom he is interacting. In many instances these painful encounters with representatives of the nondeviant world are the unwitting products of everyday interaction. Often the conventional person has meant no harm, and perhaps is not even aware that he has upset his partner in the transaction. Our investigation did not attempt to uncover whether or not the respondents saw the nondeviants as responsible for their penalizing experiences. Presumably such an interpretation of their encounters with so-called normals would only increase their feeling of commitment, and harden their antisocial sentiments. Certainly, more research is needed in this area.

In connection with the discussion of these four penalties (6–9), it was mentioned that knowledge of the criminal's identity is a necessary factor in their manifestation; and that conditions like notoriety of the deviant's activities, community size, efficiency of the communications media, and seriousness of the offense are factors here. While we have not systematically pursued this issue in this study, community size and notoriety have been discussed in relation to our finding that somewhat under half of the nonprofessional respondents lived in communities with a population of 7,499 or less where evidence of notoriety was observed. Prison tattoos were discussed as a possible identifying mark of the nonprofessional criminal. Many of the respondents in the Newfoundland sample were observed to have tattooed symbols and words on their arms and hands, and the evidence suggests that the peculiar nature of these tattoos serves as a badge of criminality in certain parts of the community.

Other arrangements were suggested as penalizing, but the data did not support these suppositions. We hypothesized that in trying to ward off inquiries about his deviant past, the nonprofessional criminal ends up hurting the feelings of the nondeviant others present in the situation. We proposed that the potential attenuation of social skills resulting from long imprisonment makes adjustment to conventional life, and especially to women and children, difficult and upsetting. It was also suggested that this same condition creates hardships in sustaining and developing interpersonal relationships. Goffman's assertion that nondeviants subtly undermine the deviant individual's usual scheme of interpreting everyday events was also examined, but it was not supported by the data.

Penalties 11 through 13 reflect the problems involved in "passing," that is, in the deviant's attempt to interact with conventional members of the community without their being aware of his deviant identity. This practice makes the non-professional criminal vulnerable to certain kinds of anxiety-producing events.

The conclusion that the arrangements discussed so far in this summary are penalizing results from the definitions of situations by the individual respondents themselves. After undergoing many penalizing experiences, the deviant begins to conclude, on the basis of retrospective thought, that life is on the whole more satisfying outside the conventional world. This recognition is simultaneously a recognition of continuance commitment to deviance.

Another potential renunciation social penalty experienced by the nonprofessional criminal is his general attitude in regard to the lack of understanding shown by nondeviants for his situation. Although a large proportion of "don't know" answers signals caution, Penalty 14 is presented as an expression of this feeling. The deviant believes that he receives more sympathy and understanding within the circle of like deviants, certain other kinds of deviants, and assorted groups of sympathizers.

When we consider Penalties 6 through 14, we seem to have at least indirect evidence for Skolnick's hypothesis that the parolee who returns to an environment which moderately accepts the prisoner's norms will be more likely to achieve parole success than one who returns to an environment which largely rejects or mostly accepts these norms.[18] It is evident from the data presented in Chapter 5 that a nonaccepting environment is penalizing. Whether or not such penalties actually cause the deviant to remain in his identity is, of course, not demonstrated here, but must await future research.

Penalty 15—the dislike of police contact with regard to suspected criminal activity—at first appeared somewhat ambiguous. Data from this study and others indicate that there is serious police harassment in only a small minority of the cases, a fact which makes such interaction nonpenalizing from one point of view. But when police contact publicizes the deviant's identity while he is attempting to gain entrance to the nondeviant world, such contact is seen as definitely penalizing. In other words, it suggests to the conventional world that a particular deviant individual has not yet reformed.

A number of other hypothetical renunciation social penalties have been presented in this chapter, but they failed to receive support from the present study or from other investigations of the nonprofessional criminal. Both Goffman and Lemert have suggested that to the degree that individual members of the community recognize the deviant and believe that his stigma will generalize to them, they will establish the necessary amount of social distance to prevent this. That no supporting evidence was found in the current study is not surprising, considering the fact that many of the nonprofessional respondents had as friends a significant number of ex-offenders. Glaser found similar results in his own survey. Female friends usually treated the released nonprofessional criminal with little distance, although there were several notable exceptions where the deviant was rejected when the girl involved learned of his unsavory past. Finally, it can be said that, in general, members of the ex-offender's family of orientation also behaved this way. In connection with this last point it was noted that feelings of shame and embarrassment may be construed as penalizing, but whether this penalty is one of renunciation or continuation is a question for future research.

Theoretically, one can expect that with extended absence there will be a certain amount of change in the content of interpersonal relationships, change which includes a general decline in the degree of intimacy. It was hypothesized that such change would be interpreted as penalizing for the ex-prisoner, but the results from the present study do not bear this out. A fair proportion of the respondents, nonprofessional and professional, noticed changes in their interpersonal relationships, but they did not define these as penalizing, a finding which appears to hold even when length of prison sentence is controlled. If further research establishes that these changes are, in fact, penalizing where sufficient length of absence has occurred, the resulting penalty will be a continuation penalty. These things would not have happened to the nonprofessional criminal if he had stayed out of trouble, and thus had not been away from others for so long.

Finally, it was suggested that being forced to accept responsibility for rearing children, for providing the necessities of life for a family, and for making family decisions is distasteful to the released nonprofessonal criminal. Although the present study did not provide supporting evidence for this hypothesis, it is considered a potential renunciation social penalty on the basis of the following reasoning: the deviant has little liking for these duties, which are conventionally expected of the husband in our society; they are interpreted as penalizing in contrast to the norms of criminal life where such responsibilities can be legitimately passed off to the distaff side of the family. Whatever evidence is produced on this theme in the future, it will always pertain only to the married minority of nonprofessional and professional criminals. Marriage, apparently, is not the deviant's idea of the good life.

Generally speaking, the professional criminal's position with respect to interpersonal relations with nondeviants was one of considerably less experience than that of the nonprofessional. Typically, he maintained few "straight" friends of any sort, which meant he had much less familiarity with the kinds of situations portrayed in the questionnaire items. Yet when he did come into contact with people in the "straight" world, he seemed to experience little anxiety over the possibility of discovery. He appeared, rather, to regard such circumstances as a challenge to his social skills, often making up plausible stories to fit the occasion. This relaxed demeanor with nondeviants was partly related to the low-risk potential associated with these transactions; the professional criminal had no major desires, as a rule, that could be frustrated should his dissembling fail.

NOTES

1. Daniel Glaser, *The Effectiveness of a Prison and Parole System,* p. 394.

2. Ibid., p. 398.

3. Perhaps the statement of this sentiment is somewhat exaggerated—really a form of righteous indignation—since many inmates apparently harbor considerable hostility and suspicion toward authority figures which persists once out of prison. See Louis Zeitoun, "Parole Supervision and Self-Determination," *Federal Probation* 26 (September 1962): 1–4.

4. Erving Goffman, *Stigma: Notes on the Management of Spoiled Identity*, pp. 30, 47; Edwin M. Lemert, *Social Pathology*, p. 65.

5. Glaser, *Effectiveness of Prison and Parole*, p. 389. Earlier in his report Glaser does mention that most inmates at the institutions he studied were aware of some loss of friends because of stigma (p. 369).

6. Glaser found that kin relationships improved with the course of imprisonment, *Effectiveness of Prison and Parole*, p. 381.

7. Some recent evidence indicates that the reaction of the family to the ex-offender varies cross-culturally. See Harold Finestone, "Reformation and Recidivism among Italian and Polish Criminal Offenders," *American Journal of Sociology* 72 (May 1967): 575–588.

8. In his life story, Robert Allerton suggests this penalty. See Tony Parker and Robert Allerton, *The Courage of His Convictions*, pp. 123–124.

9. Alfred Schutz, *Collected Papers II: Studies in Social Theory*, ed. Arvid Brodersen, pp. 38–39.

10. See Alfred Schutz, "The Homecomer," in ibid., esp. pp. 111–112.

11. To the author's knowledge, no one has seriously addressed himself to this problem. Morris found that family ties were loosened with imprisonment, but her study was not longitudinal, so this question of reestablishment of relationships could not be assessed. See Pauline Morris, *Prisoners and Their Families*, p. 297.

12. A. M. Kirkpatrick, *The Human Problems of Prison After-Care*, rev. ed., p. 5.

13. A. M. Kirkpatrick, "After-Care and the Prisoner's Aid Societies," in *Crime and its Treatment in Canada*, ed. William T. McGrath, p. 397.

14. There is also a potential continuation social penalty stemming from the observation, cited above, that the ex-offender's wife may not care to give up her own newly acquired independence. If the ex-offender finds this threatening and dis-

tasteful, it could be seen as a stimulus to try to return to a non-deviant life to avoid returning to prison and repeating the experience.

15. This renunciation penalty presumes that being responsible in the sense employed here is a cultural expectation in conventional circles, and that such an expectation does not exist in the subculture of crime as a way of life. One can be married, but the matter of responsibility in most things domestic is left to the deviant's wife.

16. Roughly one-third of Glaser's sample was married at the time of prison entry, while in England Morris found 43 percent of her sample to be married. See Glaser, *Effectiveness of Prison and Parole,* p. 368; Morris, *Prisoners,* p. 31.

17. John Bartlow Martin, *My Life in Crime: The Autobiography of a Professional Criminal,* p. 275.

18. Jerome H. Skolnick, "Toward a Developmental Theory of Parole," *American Sociological Review* 25 (August 1960): 548.

7

CONCLUSIONS AND IMPLICATIONS

There is perhaps no better concise justification for this study than the following statement by Edwin Lemert:

> Yet when all of this has been said, questions remain as to the relationship between inmate socialization and subsequent criminality on discharge from reformatories and prisons. Does new deviance spring from a continuing sense of injustice, which is reinforced by job rejections, police cognizance, and strained interaction with normals on the outside, or is it due to an acquired ideological view that this is what the world will be like when reentered? Does the latter, in turn, build into sensitivity and cause a projection of deviance expectancy in interaction, or does it lead discharged criminals to seek out companionship of delinquents, criminals and ex-convicts like themselves? On such questions research is less enlightening than it is on workings of the prison system.[1]

It is on this theoretically and empirically weak area of the study of deviance that we have focused our attention—on that phase of the deviant's career in which the transition from primary to secondary deviance or to some other mode of adjustment is made. The theory of continuance commitment has been presented and developed as a point of consolidation for past, present, and future formulations in this area of deviance research.

By way of summary we simply repeat the condensed definition of commitment developed in Chapter 2: commitment is defined as the psychological state of awareness of the relative impossibility of choosing a specified different identity or rejecting a single expectation because of the perceived imminence of the biological, psychological, and/or social penalties involved in making the switch. Empirically, our efforts have been concentrated on the social penalties involved in the attempt to regain a respectable or at least an acceptable position in conventional circles. More specifically, our aims were to discover the nature of these social penalties, and to learn why they are objectionable enough to create the feeling of commitment in the nonprofessional criminal.

It is neither necessary nor practical to recapitulate the many thoughts and findings presented in the foregoing chapters. The major results from the research conducted on Newfoundland third- and fourth-time offenders have been stated in testable, hypothetical form as renunciation social penalties Numbers 1 through 15. These are presented in the "Summary and Conclusions" sections found at the end of Chapters 4 and 6.

It is impossible to summarize adequately a developed theory, and it is imprudent to attempt to do so when a more complete statement of it is readily available. We have pointedly avoided violating this dictum so far in this book (except as a mnemonic strategy in chapter summaries), and we wish to continue to do so in this chapter. The general conceptual background for the theory was presented in Chapter 1 by reviewing the postulates underlying Lemert's theory of sociopathic behavior so that the reader might see how his work relates to contemporary notions about the deviant career. Those interested in the full theoretical statement were referred to the proper sources. In Chapter 2 a theory of commitment was presented, and its place in the deviant career as a turning point was determined.

The nonprofessional criminal may be unique: he is, perhaps, the only major type of deviant who is slow to learn about his commitment, a situation which earlier was attributed to the less inevitable quality of social penalties. This was the justification for selecting nonprofessional criminals for study. It was reasoned that if the existence of commitment-producing penalties could be demonstrated for nonprofessionals, penalties associated with forms of deviance in which these penalties are more inevitable would certainly be found.

There are, however, several aspects of the social penalties experienced by nonprofessional criminals which have not been systematically treated in the foregoing chapters. These aspects, along with the implications of all social penalties for this kind of deviance, are discussed below.

THE SOCIAL PENALTIES AND THEIR IMPLICATIONS

The fifteen renunciation social penalties presented so far have all been given some degree of support from either the present

study, another study, or both. Several other hypothetical renunciation penalties did not receive support from the current
investigation. This may be due less to their invalidity than
to their failure to manifest themselves in our rather limited
research conditions. The present study was based on small
samples of only two kinds of criminals, nonprofessional
and professional property offenders, most of whom were un-
married. Additionally, some of these penalties were formulated as a result of conversations with the respondents, and
consequently they received no systematic investigation. Because of these reservations we would also like to suggest the
following as perceived renunciation social penalties, pending
their confirmation in future research:

a) When his presence in the company of nondeviant others makes them uncomfortable, the nonprofessional
   criminal feels remorse.
b) The presence of preprison debts prevents or at least
   seriously impedes progress toward such goals in life
   as success and independence.
c) A lack of money denies the no professional criminal
   the whitewashing effect which its presence produces.
d) Nondeviant members of the community may undermine the nonprofessional criminal's usual scheme of
   interpretation of everyday events.
e) Adaptive techniques, designed to stave off discovery of
   or probing about the nonprofessional criminal's past,
   may give rise to hurt feelings on the part of nondeviants and consequent remorse on the part of the deviant.
f) Rejection by nondeviant male and female friends, because of the contamination possible from associating
   with someone with a prison record, is perceived by the

nonprofessional criminal as a renunciation social penalty.

g) Where known, the nonprofessional criminal may experience anxiety in a gathering of nondeviants because he feels they will suspect him if any money or
other item is discovered to be missing.

h) The denial of credit needed to borrow money or buy
on the installment plan, whether because of the nonprofessional criminal's prison record or because of
his unstable employment situation, is perceived as
penalizing.

i) Exploitation of the nonprofessional criminal by unscrupulous employees and company officials is perceived as a renunciation social penalty.

j) When the nonprofessional criminal is forced to take
responsibilities in his family of procreation like child
disciplining, domestic decision making, and providing
material support, he perceives these as costs.

These renunciation penalties are all seen, through the deviant's eyes, as developing from attempts to abandon criminality
as a full or supplementary livelihood or from attempts to
associate with nondeviant others. When many such events
are interpreted in this manner and when they have the effect
of impressing upon the ex-criminal that a deviant way of
life is preferable, continuance commitment will have been
reached.

Although beyond the scope of the present study, several
perceived continuation social penalties were also discovered
during the analysis. Since the ultimate recognition of commitment by any deviant depends upon his assessment of the

combined costs associated with his current identity as compared with that of a conventional member of the community, it is in the interest of future research to list these hypotheses as well.

a) When the nonprofessional criminal discovers upon his release from prison that some of his personal or family property is missing, this is perceived as penalizing.

b) When the nonprofessional criminal discovers upon his release from prison that the material and health conditions of his family of procreation have worsened considerably, he perceives this as a penalty.

c) When the nonprofessional criminal has been in prison a sufficient length of time and upon release discovers major and upsetting changes in his important interpersonal relationships, he interprets this as a continuation social penalty.

d) Where the nonprofessional criminal has difficulty sustaining old interpersonal relationships and developing new ones because of an attenuation of interpersonal skills resulting from long imprisonment, he perceives this as a social penalty.

e) Where the nonprofessional criminal returns home from a prison sentence to find that his wife has grown to be independent of him and where he sees this as threatening his role as husband, he perceives this as a continuation social penalty.

f) The shame experienced by the nonprofessional criminal as a result of his family's reactions to his deviant behavior is perceived as a penalty.

These are continuation penalties because they impress upon

the nonprofessional criminal the costs of maintaining his deviant identity.

Continuation penalties (d) and (e), it must be noted, also have possible alternative interpretations as renunciation social penalties. Thus, the deviant would presumably not have to endure either of these if he had stayed in sympathetic circles in the first instance and eschewed family responsibilities in the second. Whether they are to be labeled here as continuation or renunciation penalties cannot be determined without research into the nonprofessional criminal's actual definition of the matter. The same must be said for the first three continuation penalties, for there is always the chance of a boomerang effect resulting from the resentment produced by such experiences.

The modern attitude toward deviant behavior, manifested in renunciation social penalties, appears to have historical roots in the religious beliefs brought to North America from England during the colonial period.

> The theological views which sustained this deployment pattern have largely disappeared from the religious life of the society, but the attitudes toward deviation which were implied in the pattern are still retained in many of the institutions we have built to process and confine deviant offenders. We are still apt to visualize deviant behavior as the product of a deep-seated characterological strain in the person who enacts it, rather than as the product of the situation in which it took place, and we are still apt to treat that person as if his whole being was somehow implicated in what is often no more than a passing deviant episode.[2]

The effects of this attitude on readmission of the reformed deviant to conventional life is very complicated; the theory of commitment presented in this monograph attempts to cope with some of the factors involved.

Implications

Although we have by no means made a thorough assessment of the penalties associated with abandoning or remaining in a deviant identity, it should be apparent that no matter what one does, penalties must be endured. As we have already pointed out, remaining in the deviant identity is only the lesser of two evils when all the perceived penalties are interpreted as an aggregate. Apparently even professional criminals are aware of the not-so-desirable prospects of their chosen way of life. Robert Allerton illustrates this in the following reply to a question from Tony Parker about where he expects to be at age sixty-five:

> But on the eve of my life-time, do you mean, where shall I be then? . . . My common sense—which I get disgusted with, I hate my common sense—tells me I'll still be penniless and ignorant, just as ignorant as I am now, because of my indolence and all the other things I lack. Or maybe I shall be stinking it out in some prison somewhere, doing a fifteen stretch, wits dulled, mind full of bitterness . . . you can't expect me to follow common sense that far, that's why I hate my common sense when it starts leading to things like that. One doesn't dig very deeply into the future, you know, one tries just to live for the day and have no regrets.[3]

If this single case can be taken as an accurate depiction of the professional criminal's outlook on life, then that of the nonprofessional, however he reacts to his commitment, must be no less dismal.

On the other hand, even a successful reintegration into conventional living is fraught with hazards and penalties. Generally, these are variations on the theme of trying to keep one's deviant past secret, an endeavor which apparently knows no end. For exposure can have disastrous effects, far beyond mere embarrassment. As was mentioned in our Introduction, Canadians within a year learned through their mass media about two political figures, one a Member of Parliament and the other a town councillor, whose criminal records were suddenly brought to light, promoting a great deal of uncertainty in the future political career of one and bringing about the resignation of the other.[4]

It is in the fact that there are penalties associated with both deviant and nondeviant modes of life that we anchor the following practical suggestions. These suggestions are based on the general strategy of manipulating the balance of penalties in such a way as to make the pursuit of a conventional identity the less-evil choice instead of the deviant identity.

One obvious tactic is to decrease notoriety wherever possible. The author has noted with admiration that a major newspaper in St. John's, *The Evening Telegram,* has shunned commercial interests to the extent of usually omitting the names of people prosecuted in Magistrate's Court. If more community newspapers and other mass media followed this example, the possibility of several renunciation social penalties discussed in this book would decrease, though certainly not disappear.

The very fact that the criminal record exists in an official file somewhere is a threat to some proportion of reformed or would-be reformed deviants. In this respect, the Canadian Parliament has recently passed the Criminal Records Act, which erases summary convictions after three years and indictable convictions after five years. This is a step in the right direction.[5] Evidence from the present study, although hardly strong enough alone to be the basis for such recommendations, suggests that even a lesser number of years between the last crime and destruction of the criminal record would be desirable. A large-scale study of Canadian criminals similar to that of Glaser's in the United States could produce useful data which might facilitate decision-making in this area.

Additional schooling of all sorts should be made available to incarcerated criminals.[6] The acquisition of trade skills, high school diplomas, and even university degrees are investments which would help commit the deviant to a respectable identity.[7] A variety of related recommendations are made by Glaser, including the availability of loans and unemployment insurance for released prisoners.[8] All of these can be seen as directly or indirectly supporting the ex-offender's nondeviant self-image as they reduce the penalties normally associated with renouncing one's deviant identity.

Since our recommendations derive from the assumption that groups of penalties are subjectively weighed against each other, the suggestion that society increase the continuation penalties, whatever they may be, merits consideration.[9] For example, if future research can demonstrate that resentment is not always associated with such a strategy and that the criminal remembers the penalizing experience when he is about to deviate in the future, then *more stringent* penal practices may be called for, providing public opinion on this issue is not too badly violated. As our results suggest, however, there is often the possibility of a boomerang effect, whereby these practices are perceived as examples of injustice, leading then to resentment and continued deviance.

Unfortunately, little can apparently be done about penalties of the kind discussed in Chapters 5 and 6. Devices which cut down notoriety will always help, but they can never eliminate the unsettling events associated with passing. However, it may be that as the reformed deviant comes to be more committed to a conventional identity he develops psychological and other means for dealing with these incidents, means which exclude him from the judgments made by others and which arm him against the potential probing we discussed earlier. Time here serves as a facilitating factor: the greater the number of years after release from prison, the less likely it is that the ex-offender will be expected to remember and talk about that particular period of his life with any degree of accuracy. One can always rely at this stage on the acceptable excuse that "I just don't remember." Halfway houses, John Howard Society supervisors, and parole officers can help the newly released inmate to acquire the capacity to cope with the exigencies often found in social relations.

These suggestions are based upon the fact that the self-degrading commitment experienced by a proportion of non-professional criminals is so undesirable as to be motivating. They are based on the assumption that by altering the balance of penalties in certain ways a conventional identity will become the choice of lesser evil. The practitioner, i.e., the social worker, the parole officer, the clergyman, must always remember, however, that it is the deviant's *interpretation* of the balance of many kinds of penalties as gleaned from interaction with others and from learned anticipations that must be altered. The deviant must be made to see that the balance has changed (and probably in many cases, he must be shown the actual nature of the balance before change). Here is where the practitioner plays one of his most important roles.

COMMITMENT AS A CAUSE
OF DEVIANCE

The present study has been exploratory in scope, intended only to identify various renunciation social penalties and to show the way they might create the psychological state of commitment. It is plain that more controlled research is needed to obtain conclusive evidence that such penalties actually cause further deviance. Such research would take hypothetical social penalties like those presented here and look for their absence among a control group of ex-offenders who have successfully integrated themselves into a conventional walk of life.[10] By way of caution to those who might wish to take up such a project, it is probably possible to carry out only in a metropolis. Inquiries even in a city the size of St. John's revealed that many ex-offenders who would help make up such a control group had left town, never to return. Glaser's survey, on the other hand, shows that residents of large cities do not seem to leave them after their release from prison, in spite of certain imminent penalties involved.[11]

The causal model which the present theory of commitment demands is that suggested by Robert MacIver. Cause for him is the definition of the situation, which we have defined as the personal interrelation and interpretation of the social, psychological, physical, and physiological elements in the ongoing situation.[12] Outside of the immediate short-range goals which lead one to enter a setting, the psychological components of the situation are basically predispositional in nature. The usage of the term "predisposition" follows that of Campbell.[13] He limits his statement to acquired states, stressing the importance of the fact that predispositions (or as he calls them, "acquired behavioral dispositions") are enduring and remain dormant until "activated" by situational stimuli. When activated, these products of past experience impinge upon our awareness, equip us with a specific view of the world, and guide behavior in the immediate present. Values, attitudes, bits of knowledge, memory, habits, and meanings of all kinds have predispositional qualities about them.

Actually our causal model is two-phased. First, we are interested in explaining how the predisposition of commitment evolves. It can be hypothesized that this state develops through past experience or through what has been called the "retrospective definition," in which the individual sums up and defines the many penalties endured and anticipated, culminating in the feeling of commitment.[14] According to this model, arrangements cause commitment only after they have been defined as penalizing by the deviant. Such a definition is always retrospective in that the individual concerned gradually realizes, after reassessing past experiences and thinking about his future (if he dares do such a thing), that the way of least resistance lies with continued deviance.

This points to the second phase of the model, in which the objective is to explain situated behavior relating to one's deviance and commitment. The cognitive state of continuance commitment, when activated by the appropriate stimuli in the setting, is one of the predispositions or psychological factors in the person's definition of the situation. As a view of the world it contributes to the interpretation of that setting, and that interpretation serves as the immediate guide for subsequent behavior. Thus, the nonprofessional criminal who is considering getting married and having a family may (in situations where matrimony is actually discussed with his intended or reflected upon by him alone) suddenly find himself also contemplating the many penalties associated with abandoning his criminal identity—a strategy that may seem necessary at that time. This activated predisposition serves to direct his behavior, leading him either to a rejection of marriage or a redefinition of the renunciation penalties which would permit him to reject his deviant status after all.

Framing the matter this way has another advantage. The penalties, whether physiological, psychological, or social, will not necessarily occur in the same combinations in every form of deviance or even appear at all, because the arrangements which produce them may be different. This was evident earlier when we pointed out the major differences between the nonprofessional criminal and other kinds of deviants in this regard. Consequently, there will be different definitions of the situation, both ongoing and retrospective, associated with the various forms of deviance. But when the specified conditions are met, these differing meanings will all lead to the state of commitment. Commitment, then, has a basic set of characteristics recognizable in all forms of deviance, but the combined renunciation penalties that produce it and the interpretation of these by the people involved will vary by form of deviance.

This is, perhaps, no better illustrated than in the comparison between penalties leading to commitment among nonprofessional criminals and those leading to commitment among the mentally ill. The social penalties arising from interpersonal relations between the nonprofessional criminal and nondeviants are, of course, odious. But in addition, the deviant sometimes feels that he is not wanted among non-deviants because they do not respect him, they suspect he may steal from them, they fear he will contaminate their reputations. The conventional members of the community simply prefer not to have such a person around—even though, being thus ostracized, he is still expected to refrain from further deviant behavior.

Contrast this situation with the penalties endured by mental patients and ex-mental patients. Here, too, there are no doubt obvious social penalties arising out of interaction with normals. But while the patient or ex-patient views these penalties as objectionable, he also views them as forcing him to continue as a deviant. The mentally ill are apparently tolerated in conventional circles, but only if they act "crazy." For some proportion of nonprofessional criminals there appears to be no acceptance in conventional circles, a situation which forces them to remain outside in deviant settings. There is evidence that the mentally ill *are* tolerated in conventional circles, but only if they act out their expected role—one which demands the feigning of lunacy.[15] But in either case these two categories of deviants are committed to their identities.

In closing we must emphasize that the research strategy indicated for those studying continuance commitment among deviants should follow MacIver's general formulation: the delimitation of the phenomena being studied in order to arrive at a project of manageable size.[16] Each form of deviance must be studied in order to sort out the various differences in associated penalties and their interpretations. There will be common elements among these forms, but there will also be important differences—differences which will enhance our theoretical understanding of commitment and facilitate the work of practitioners.[17]

NOTES

1. Edwin H. Lemert, *Human Deviance, Social Problems, and Social Control,* pp. 46–47.

2. Kai T. Erikson, *Wayward Puritans,* p. 198.

3. Tony Parker and Robert Allerton, *The Courage of His Convictions,* p. 189.

4. *The Evening Telegram* (St. John's, Newfoundland), 18 January 1967, p. 1; ibid., 18 April 1967, p. 1.

5. The deviant's record is erased from the date of his last conviction.

6. The author is well aware of the problem of motivation involved here. Perhaps it is an even greater drawback to the implementation of such a strategy than the reluctance of members of the community to support it through increased taxation.

7. A recent innovation is that of Oregon inmates attending university-level courses within the prison given by faculty members of Oregon State University. These courses, which are inspiring enough to motivate these prisoners to study harder than conventional students, can lead to an accredited degree. See *The Christian Science Monitor,* 16 June 1967, p. 1.

8. Daniel Glaser, *The Effectiveness of a Prison and Parole System,* chap. 16.

9. Throughout all of this discussion an emphasis upon rewards, where they are not simply the opposite of penalties, is also in order. Since the present study did not concern itself with this aspect of behavior, we have nothing new to add in the way of recommendations of this nature.

10. Parolees are, of course, the best respondents for such an

undertaking since that status indicates that, statistically speaking, those in it are least likely to recidivate.

11. Glaser, *Effectiveness of Prison and Parole,* p. 376.

12. Robert M. MacIver, *Social Causation,* chap. 11. He actually uses the term "dynamic assessment" for our idea of the definition of the situation.

13. Donald T. Campbell, "Social Attitudes and Other Acquired Behavioral Dispositions," in *Psychology: A Study of a Science,* ed. Sigmund Koch, 6:94–172.

14. The notion of retrospective definition was developed by Florian Znaniecki, *Cultural Sciences,* p. 251. For a further discussion of the interrelationship between retrospective definitions and definitions of the situation, see Robert A. Stebbins, "A Theory of the Definition of the Situation," *The Canadian Review of Sociology and Anthropology* 4 (August 1967): 161–168.

15. This view of the societal reaction to the mentally ill is emphasized by, among others, Thomas J. Scheff, *Being Mentally Ill,* pp. 84–96.

16. MacIver, *Social Causation,* p. 378.

17. This is basically the same strategy proposed by Glaser and Strauss in arriving at a grounded formal or general theory. See Barney G. Glaser and Anselm L. Strauss, *Awareness of Dying,* pp. 276–280.

BIBLIOGRAPHY

Books

Becker, Howard S. *Outsiders: Studies in the Sociology of Deviance.* New York: The Free Press, 1963.

————, ed. *The Other Side.* New York: The Free Press, 1964.

Bloch, Herbert and Niederhoffer, Arthur. *The Gang.* New York: Philosophical Library, 1958.

Blum, Richard, et al. *Utopiates.* New York, Atherton Press, 1964.

Brehm, Jack W., and Cohen, A. R. *Explorations in Cognitive Dissonance.* New York: John Wiley & Sons, 1962.

Chein, Isidor, et al. *The Road to H.* New York: Basic Books, 1964.

Clinard, Marshall B. *Sociology of Deviant Behavior.* New York: Holt, Rinehart & Winston, 1958.

Cloward, Richard A. and Ohlin, Lloyd E. *Delinquency and Opportunity.* New York: The Free Press, 1960.

Cressey, Donald R. *Other People's Money*. Glencoe, Ill.: The Free Press, 1953.

Erikson, Kai T. *The Wayward Puritans*. New York: John Wiley & Sons, 1966.

Festinger, Leon. *Conflict, Decision, and Dissonance*. Stanford: Stanford University Press, 1964.

Festinger, Leon; Riecken, Henry W., Jr.; and Schachter, Stanley. *When Prophecy Fails*. Minneapolis: University of Minnesota Press, 1956.

Garfinkle, Harold *Studies in Ethnomethodology*. Englewood Cliffs, N.J.: Prentice-Hall, 1967.

Gibbons, Don C. *Society, Crime, and Criminal Careers*. Englewood Cliffs, N.J.: Prentice-Hall, 1968.

Glaser, Barney G. and Strauss, Anselm L. *Awareness of Dying*. Chicago: Aldine Publishing Co., 1965.

Glaser, Daniel. *The Effectiveness of a Prison and Parole System*. Indianapolis: The Bobbs-Merrill Co., 1964.

Goffman, Erving. *Asylums*. Garden City, N.Y.: Doubleday and Co., 1961.

———. *Encounters*. Indianapolis: The Bobbs-Merrill Co., 1961.

———. *Behavior in Public Places*. New York: The Free Press, 1963.

———. *Stigma: Notes on the Management of Spoiled Identity*. Englewood Cliffs, N.J.: Prentice-Hall, 1963.

———. *Interaction Ritual*. Chicago: Aldine Publishing Co., 1967.

Grinker, Roy R. and Spiegel, John P. *Men Under Stress*. New York: McGraw-Hill Book Co., 1945.

Hovland, Carl I., et al., *The Order of Presentation in Persuasion*. New Haven: Yale University Press, 1957.

Hughes, Everett C. *Men and Their Work.* New York: The Free Press, 1958.

Ilfeld, Fred, Jr. and Lauer, Roger. *Social Nudism in America.* New Haven: College and University Press, 1964.

Johnson, Elmer Hubert. *Crime, Correction, and Society.* Homewood, Ill.: The Dorsey Press, 1964.

Jones, Edward E. *Ingratiation.* New York: Appleton-Century-Crofts, 1964.

Krech, David; Crutchfield, Richard S.; and Ballachey, Egerton L. *Individual in Society.* New York: McGraw-Hill Book Co., 1962.

Lemert, Edwin M. *Human Deviance, Social Problems, and Social Control.* Englewood Cliffs, N.J.: Prentice-Hall, 1967.

————. *Social Pathology.* New York: McGraw-Hill Book Co., 1951.

Lincoln, C. Eric. *The Black Muslims in America.* Boston: Beacon Press, 1961.

Lindesmith, Alfred R. and Strauss, Anselm L. *Social Psychology.* 3d ed. New York: Holt, Rinehart & Winston, 1968.

Lofland, John. *Doomsday Cult.* Englewood Cliffs, N.J.: Prentice-Hall, 1966.

MacIver, Robert M. *Social Causation.* New York: Harper & Row, Publishers, 1964.

Martin, J. P. *Offenders as Employees.* London: Macmillan & Co. 1962.

Martin, John Bartlow. *My Life in Crime.* New York: Harper & Bros., 1952.

Matza, David, *Delinquency and Drift.* New York: John Wiley & Sons, 1964.

Merton, Robert K. *Social Theory and Social Structure*. Rev. ed. New York: The Free Press, 1957.

Morris, Pauline. *Prisoners and Their Families*. New York: Hart Publishing Co., 1965.

Newcomb, Theodore M. *The Acquaintance Process*. New York: Holt, Rinehart & Winston, 1961.

Nosow, Sigmund and Form, William H., eds. *Man, Work, and Society*. New York: Basic Books, 1962.

Parker, Tony and Allerton, Robert. *The Courage of His Convictions*. London: Hutchinson & Co., 1962.

Parsons, Talcott. *The Social System*. New York: The Free Press, 1951.

Polsky, Ned. *Hustlers, Beats, and Others*. Chicago: Aldine Publishing Co., 1967.

Scheff, Thomas J. *Being Mentally Ill*. Chicago: Aldine Publishing Co., 1966.

Schelling, Thomas C. *A Strategy of Conflict*. Cambridge, Mass.: Harvard University Press, 1960.

Schur, Edwin M. *Crimes Without Victims*. Englewood Cliffs, N.J.: Prentice-Hall, 1965.

Schutz, Alfred. *Collected Papers II: Studies in Social Theory*. Edited by Arvid Brodersen. The Hague: Martinus Nijhoff, 1964.

Shaw, Clifford, R. *The Jack Roller*. Chicago: University of Chicago Press, 1930.

————. *Brothers in Crime*. Chicago: University of Chicago Press, 1938.

Skolnick, Jerome H., *Justice Without Trial*. New York: John Wiley & Sons, 1966.

Slocum, Walter, L. *Occupational Careers.* Chicago: Aldine Publishing Co., 1966.

Sutherland, Edwin, ed. *The Professional Thief.* Chicago: University of Chicago Press, 1937.

White, Robert W. *The Abnormal Personality.* 2d ed. New York: The Ronald Press Co., 1956.

Wilkins, Leslie T. *Social Deviance: Social Policy, Action, and Research.* Englewood Cliffs, N.J.: Prentice-Hall, 1965.

Znaniecki, Florian, *Cultural Sciences.* Urbana, Ill.: University of Illinois Press, 1952.

Articles

Abramson, E., et al. "Social Power and Commitment." *American Sociological Review,* 23 (1958): 15–22.

Argyle, Michael and Kendon, Adam. "Experimental Analysis of Social Performance." In *Advances in Experimental Social Psychology,* edited by Leonard Berkowitz. Vol. 3. New York: Academic Press, 1967.

Ball, John C. "Reliability and Validity of Interview Data Obtained from 59 Narcotic Drug Addicts." *American Journal of Sociology* 72 (May 1967): 650–654.

Bateson, Gregory. "Bali: The Value System of a Steady State." In *Social Structure: Studies Presented to A. R. Radcliffe-Brown,* edited by Meyer Fortes. New York: Russell and Russell, 1963.

Becker, Howard S. "The Professional Dance Musician and His Audience." *American Journal of Sociology* 57 (September 1951): 136–144.

———. "The Career of the Chicago Public School Teacher." *American Journal of Sociology* 57 (1952): 470–477.

————. "Notes on the Concept of Commitment." *American Journal of Sociology* 66 (1960): 32–40.

————. "Marihuana Use and Social Control." In *Human Behavior and Social Processes,* edited by Arnold M. Rose. Boston: Houghton Mifflin Co., 1962.

————. "History, Culture, and Subjective Experience: An Exploration of the Social Bases of Drug-Induced Experiences." *Journal of Health and Social Behavior* 8 (September 1967): 163–176.

Becker, Howard S. and Strauss, Anselm L. "Careers, Personality, and Adult Socialization." *American Journal of Sociology* 62 (1956): 253–263.

Bittner, Egon. "The Police on Skid-Row." *American Sociological Review* 32 (October 1967): 699–715.

Burma, John H. "Self-Tattooing among Delinquents." *Sociology and Social Research* 43 (May–June 1959): 341–345.

Cahnman, Werner J. "The Stigma of Obesity." *The Sociological Quarterly* 9 (Summer, 1968): 283–299.

Campbell, Donald T. "Social Attitudes and Other Acquired Behavioral Dispositions." In *Psychology: A Study of a Science,* edited by Sigmund Koch. Vol. 6. New York: McGraw-Hill Book Co., 1963.

Christian Science Monitor, 16 June 1967, p. 1.

Clark, John P., et al. "Polygraph and Interview Validation of Self-Reported Deviant Behavior." *American Sociological Review* 31 (August 1966): 516–523.

Cohen, Albert K., "The Study of Social Disorganization and Deviant Behavior." In *Sociology Today: Problems and Prospects,* edited by Robert K. Merton, Leonard Broom, and Leonard S. Cottrell, Jr. New York: Basic Books, 1959.

————. "The Sociology of the Deviant Act." *American Sociological Review* 30 (February 1965): 5–14.

Cormier, Bruno M., et al. "The Natural History of Criminality and Some Tentative Hypotheses." *The Canadian Journal of Corrections* 1 (July 1959).

DeLamater, John. "On the Nature of Deviance." *Social Forces* 46 (Fall 1968): 445–455.

Dohrenwend, Bruce P., and Chin-Shong, Edwin. "Social Status and Attitudes toward Psychological Disorder." *American Sociological Review* 32 (June 1967): 417–433.

Erikson, Kai T. "Notes on the Sociology of Deviance." In *The Other Side,* edited by Howard S. Becker. New York: The Free Press, 1964.

The Evening Telegram (St. John's, Newfoundland), 16 January 1967, p. 1.

————, 18 January 1967, p. 1.

————, 18 April 1967, p. 1.

————, 13 September 1967, p. 35.

Finestone, Harold. "Reformation and Recidivism among Italian and Polish Criminal Offenders." *American Journal of Sociology* 72 (May 1967): 575–588.

Garfinkle, Harold. "Conditions of Successful Degradation Ceremonies." *American Journal of Sociology* 61 (March 1956): 420–424.

Gerard, Harold B. "Deviation, Conformity, and Commitment." In *Current Studies in Social Psychology,* edited by Ivan D. Steiner and Martin Fishbein. New York: Holt, Rinehart & Winston, 1965.

Gillies, Hunter. "Murder in the West of Scotland." *British Journal of Psychiatry* 111 (November 1965): 1087–1094.

Glaser, Daniel. "Criminality Theories and Behavioral Images." *American Journal of Sociology* 61 (March 1956): 433–444.

Goffman, Erving. "On Face Work." *Psychiatry* 18 (August 1955): 213–231.

Harvey, Edward. "Social Change and the Jazz Musician." *Social Forces* 46 (September 1967): 34–42.

Haug, Marie R., and Sussman, Marvin B. "The Second Career— Variant of a Sociological Concept." Paper read at the 61st Annual Meeting of the American Sociological Association, September 1966, Miami Beach, Florida.

Head, Jerry W. "Job Finding for Prisoners." *Federal Probation* 16 (March 1952): 20–25.

Horwood, Harold. *The Evening Telegram* (St. John's, Newfoundland), 4 April 1967, p. 23.

Kanter, Rosabeth Moss. "Commitment and Social Organization." *American Sociological Review* 33 (August 1968): 499–517.

Kinch, John W. "A Formalized Theory of the Self-Concept." *American Journal of Sociology* 68 (January 1963): 481–486.

Kirkpatrick, A. M. "After-Care and the Prisoner's Aid Societies." In *Crime and Its Treatment in Canada,* edited by William T. McGrath. Toronto: Macmillan & Co., 1965.

Kitsuse, John I. "Societal Reaction to Deviant Behavior." In *The Other Side,* edited by Howard S. Becker. New York: The Free Press, 1964.

Kornhauser, William. "Social Bases of Political Commitment." In *Human Behavior and Social Processes,* edited by Arnold M. Rose. Boston: Houghton Mifflin Co., 1962.

Landy, David and Singer, Sara E. "The Social Organization of a Club for Former Mental Patients." *Human Relations* 14 (February 1961): 31–41.

Lewin, Kurt. "Group Decision and Social Change." In *Readings in Social Psychology,* 3d ed., edited by Eleanor E. Maccoby, Theodore M. Newcomb, and Eugene L. Hartley. New York: Holt, Rinehart & Winston, 1958.

Lofland, John and Stark, Rodney. "Becoming a World Saver." *American Sociological Review* 30 (December 1965): 862–875.

Lykke, Arthur. "Attitudes of Bonding Companies Toward Probationers and Parolees." *Federal Probation* 21 (December 1957): 36–38.

McSally, Bernard F. "Finding Jobs for Released Offenders." *Federal Probation* 24 (June 1960): 12–17.

Mitchell, John. "Cons, Square-Johns, and Rehabilitation." In *Role Theory: Concepts and Research,* edited by Bruce J. Biddle and Edwin J. Thomas. New York: John Wiley & Sons, 1966.

Phillips, Derek L. "Education, Psychiatric Sophistication, and the Rejection of Mentally Ill Help-Seekers." *The Sociological Quarterly* 8 (Winter 1967): 122–132.

Piliavin, Irving and Briar, Scott. "Police Encounters with Juveniles." *American Journal of Sociology* 70 (September 1964): 206–214.

Pineo, Peter C. and Porter, John. "Occupational Prestige in Canada." *The Canadian Review of Sociology and Anthropology* 4 (February 1967): 24–40.

Ray, Marsh B. "The Cycle of Abstinence and Relapse among Heroin Addicts." In *The Other Side,* edited by Howard S. Becker. New York: The Free Press, 1964.

Rooney, Elizabeth A. and Gibbons, Don C. "Social Reactions to 'Crimes without Victims.' " *Social Problems* 13 (Spring 1966): 400–410.

Sampson, Harold; Messinger, Sheldon L.; and Towne, Robert D. "The Mental Hospital and Marital Family Ties." In *The Other Side,* edited by Howard S. Becker. New York: The Free Press, 1964.

Schwartz, Richard D. and Skolnick, Jerome H. "Two Studies of

Legal Stigma." In *The Other Side,* edited by Howard S. Becker. New York: The Free Press, 1964.

Scott, P. D., et al. "Delinquency and the Amphetamines." *British Journal of Psychiatry* 111 (September 1965): 865–875.

Simmons, J. L. "Public Stereotypes of Deviants." *Social Problems* 13 (Fall 1965): 223–232.

Skolnick, Jerome H. "Toward a Developmental Theory of Parole." *American Sociological Review* 25 (August 1960): 542–549.

Stebbins, Robert A. "Career: The Subjective Approach." *The Sociological Quarterly* 11 (Winter 1970): 32–49.

————. "The Conflict Between Musical and Commercial Values in the Minneapolis Jazz Community." *Proceedings of the Minnesota Academy of Science* 30 (1962): 75–79.

————. "Class, Status, and Power among Jazz and Commercial Musicians." *The Sociological Quarterly* 7 (Spring 1966): 197–213.

————. "Commitment, Attachment, and Deviance." Paper read at the 31st Annual Meeting of the Midwest Sociological Society, April 1967, Des Moines, Iowa.

————. "On Misunderstanding the Concept of Commitment: A Theoretical Clarification." *Social Forces* 48 (June 1970): 526–529.

————. "Studying the Definition of the Situation: Theory and Field Research Strategies." *The Canadian Review of Sociology and Anthropology* 6 (November 1969): 193–211.

————. "A Theory of the Definition of the Situation." *The Canadian Review of Sociology and Anthropology* 4 (August 1967): 148–164.

Stryker, Sheldon. "Conditions of Accurate Role-Taking: A Test of Mead's Theory." In *Human Behavior and Social Processes,* edited by Arnold M. Rose. Boston: Houghton Mifflin Co., 1962.

Trasler, Gordon. "The Social Relations of Persistent Offenders." In *The Sociological Review Monograph No. 9: Sociological Studies in the British Penal Services,* edited by Paul Halmos. Keele: University of Keele, June 1965, pp. 87–97.

Wechsler, Henry. "The Ex-Patient Organization." *Journal of Social Issues* 16 (1960): 47–53.

Wheeler, Stanton. "Socialization in Correctional Institutions." *American Sociological Review* 26 (October 1961): 697–712.

Yablonsky, Lewis. "The Anticriminal Society: Synanon." *Federal Probation* 26 (February 1962): 50–57.

Zeitoun, Louis. "Parole Supervision and Self-Determination." *Federal Probation* 26 (September 1962).

Other

DeWitt, Robert and Wadel, Cato. "Resettlement and Redevelopment: A Study of Notre Dame Bay." St. John's, Newfoundland: Institute of Social and Economic Research, Memorial University of Newfoundland, forthcoming.

Faris, James. "Cat Harbour: A Newfoundland Fishing Settlement." Newfoundland Social and Economic Studies, No. 3. St. John's, Newfoundland: Institute of Social and Economic Research, Memorial University of Newfoundland, 1966.

Firestone, Melvin M. "Brothers and Rivals: Patrilocality in Savage Cove." Newfoundland Social and Economic Studies, No. 5. St. John's, Newfoundland: Institute of Social and Economic Research, Memorial University of Newfoundland, 1967.

Kirkpatrick, A. M. "The Human Problems of Prison After-Care." Rev. ed. Toronto: The John Howard Society of Ontario, 1962.

Melichercik, John. "Employment Problems of Former Offenders." Ottawa: The Canadian Welfare Council, Delinquency and Crime Division, May 1955.

Miller, Frank P. "Parole and the Community." Address delivered at the Annual Meeting of the John Howard Society of Windsor, Ontario, February 1961.

Paine, Robert. "Manpower Mobility Study, Summer, 1967, Newfoundland Section." Ottawa: Canadian Centre for Community Studies, 1967.

"Report for the Canadian Committee on Corrections." St. John's, Newfoundland: The Corrections Committee, The John Howard Society of Newfoundland, 1967.

Szwed, John. "Private Cultures and Public Imagery." Newfoundland Social and Economic Studies, no. 2. St. John's, Newfoundland: Institute of Social and Economic Research, Memorial University of Newfoundland, 1966.

INDEX